A DEALER'S RECORD

Agnew's 1967-81

Claude Gellée, called Le Lorrain, *The Judgement of Paris*,
43¾×58¾ inches, National Gallery of Art, Washington,
Ailsa Mellon Bruce Fund, 1969.

A DEALER'S RECORD
Agnew's 1967-81

BARRIE & JENKINS
London Melbourne Sydney Auckland Johannesburg

Barrie & Jenkins Limited
An imprint of the Hutchinson Group
3 Fitzroy Square, London W1P 6JD

Hutchinson Group (Australia) Pty Ltd
30–32 Cremorne Street, Richmond South, Victoria 3121
PO Box 151, Broadway, New South Wales 2007

Hutchinson Group (NZ) Ltd
32–34 View Road, PO Box 40-086, Glenfield, Auckland 10

Hutchinson Group (SA) (Pty) Ltd
PO Box 337, Bergvlei 2012, South Africa

First published 1981
© Thos. Agnew & Sons Limited 1981

Designed by Roger Walker

Computerset in Bembo
by MFK Graphic Systems (Typesetting) Ltd, Saffron Walden, Essex
Printed in Great Britain by Fakenham Press Ltd
Colour separations by Fotographics Ltd

ISBN 0-09-146200-2

Contents

Introduction

JULIAN AGNEW

This book, *A Dealer's Record: Agnew's 1967–81*, has been compiled to illustrate the experience of one London-based firm of fine art dealers over a period of thirteen years. The period chosen is an arbitrary one. Agnew's was founded in 1817 and the history of its first 150 years has been told elsewhere.[1] The present book takes the story from the 1967 anniversary to the present day by means of a photographic record of some of the greatest works of art which have passed through the firm's hands during that period. Interspersed with these are detailed articles by art-historians which deal in depth with eight of the outstanding paintings which have been bought and sold by Agnew's since 1967. As a postscript there is added the story of the sale of one picture, the Velasquez *Juan de Pareja*, a masterwork which narrowly failed to come into Agnew's possession.

Naturally such a record is limited by the nature of the firm of Agnew's and its activities over the period in question. Agnew's is still a family business, managed and owned by the descendants of Thomas Agnew. It specializes in Old Master paintings from the thirteenth to the nineteenth century and in English pictures of all periods, and it is with these two fields and the related ones of Old Master drawings and English watercolours that the greater part of this record is concerned. Since 1967 two new areas of interest have been added to these traditional ones – Persian miniatures and European sculpture, and these are featured in the book. Though the experience of one specialized firm in the late 1960s and the decade of the 1970s can only represent a limited section of the art market, there are nevertheless patterns discernible in this record which illustrate not only the history of Agnew's but of the market as a whole in a time of unprecedented change and interest.

The art market in this period has been dominated by one economic phenomenon – inflation. While it has long been recognized that the supply of great works of art is fixed – indeed, declining, as more and more pass into museums from which they cannot re-emerge – the coincidence of a short-term pattern of the rapidly falling value of money superimposed on the long-term pattern of a dwindling supply has had the effect of increasing dramatically the value of all works of art. Not that the spectacle of high prices in the art market is in itself anything new, as the history of the quarter-century before 1914 shows. What has been unprecedented is the *rate* of increase during the last decade and a half, as a growing demand fed by an ever-expanding supply of money and an ever more limited supply of objects has created a spiral of prices. Hence, in 1967 no work of art had ever been sold for more than £1 million, whereas by 1981 prices of several millions are becoming almost commonplace. The doctrine of 'art as an investment', in itself merely part of the age-old response to inflation which seeks protection from the declining value of paper money in objects of 'real' value, has brought into the art market new characters: the collector-dealer, in fact neither one nor the other, who as one commentator put it, 'buys noisily but sells quietly'; the pension fund seeking to protect its future beneficiaries by diversifying the investment of its huge cash flow; the street-market stallholder who can sell almost any junk on the basis that it is old and therefore precious. But where there is boom, there can also be bust, and the art market is as susceptible to the laws of economics as any other. The collector who has bought without discrimination, the auctioneer who has over-promoted his goods, the dealer who has overbought as he chases the inflationary spiral upwards, all may find themselves in trouble as the fragile and volatile art market turns against them. Even the general public, fascinated by the stories of rags to riches in the sale-room as record after record is claimed, is at the same time repelled by the identification of aesthetic with monetary values.

This seesaw of success and failure is well illustrated in the years in question. From 1967 to 1974 was a period of boom, with the pressure of money in the UK forcing prices in areas in which English collectors specialized to ever new heights. The mild recession of 1971–2 passed almost unnoticed but the bust of 1974–5 came with a vengeance. Auctioneers had to find new sources of income, few dealers did more than break even, and many collectors left the market never to return. Then in 1976 the inflationary spiral set in again, reaching a peak in Europe in 1979 and toppling over into recession in 1980. Meanwhile, in the USA, the flight from the dollar into the art market had started in the mid 'seventies, parallelling the flight from the pound of the first half of the decade, giving a new twist to the inflationary spiral and suggesting that the centre of the art market, so long in London, was rapidly moving to New York.

The competition for goods in times of inflation, whether with auctioneers or other dealers, has been intense, sometimes even vicious, and no less difficult has been the constant need to adapt to new and ever-increasing price levels. Inflation has forced companies to identify the best use of capital, whilst the swings of the economic cycle have demanded intelligent anticipation of rapidly changing situations. The growth of the art market and increased public interest have brought with them growing governmental intervention, both in the shape of Value Added Tax, imposed on the market in 1973, and in the threat of a wealth tax. Concern for the national heritage has meant that those professionally involved in the art market have had to walk a tight-rope between their desire to support a heritage policy in the United Kingdom and the necessity of recognizing the hard facts of the market, and this tight-rope has, under inflationary pressures, come increasingly close to snapping. Against this background Agnew's has had to look for new areas in which to buy and for new clients to whom it can sell, as the number of first-class objects in the traditional areas has decreased and the power of the UK market has steadily declined.

While the main reasons for the sale of great works of art remain, as they always were, death or family division, and are therefore outside a dealer's control, there is a certain sense in which a dealer can contribute to the changes in the pattern of the market caused by fluctuations of taste and economic circumstances. Certainly the great works of the Renaissance both in Italy and in the north of Europe have an acknowledged importance beyond the influence of changing tastes; for example, from Italy the Gentile da Fabriano, the Ruskin Madonna, the Sassetta, the Venetian masters of the Cinquecento, and from the north the Baldung and the Gerard David, all of which are included in the pages of this record. Equally the great names of the eighteenth century (many of them also represented in this record), Tiepolo, Canaletto and Guardi in Italy, Watteau, Boucher, Fragonard and Pater in France, are beyond the influence of fashion. But major works by all these artists are today scarce, and often, following the example of art-historians and organizers of great exhibitions, the market has had to look elsewhere for new interests. One such interest, both art-historical and commercial, is shown by the emphasis in this record on the Italian seventeenth century, for it includes two most important contrasting examples of Annibale Carracci's work, a tender and lyrical Gentileschi and no less than three superb Guido Renis, as well as pictures by Domenichino and Guercino. Such a list of Seicento artists would not of course have surprised the collectors and dealers of the age of Reynolds, but, having passed through a trough of neglect in the nineteenth century, only since 1945 have they regained the fame that they once enjoyed. Initially this was due to the work of art-historians, whose researches and teaching caused a whole generation of museum directors, private collectors and dealers to reassess this long-neglected field. The lack of first-class examples in most major museums outside Italy, combined with the availability of such examples in private collections old and new, has created a demand which has been reinforced by a series of exhibitions, of which Agnew's own loan show in 1973, 'England and the Seicento', was one. The result has been a vigorous and active market in this particular field, encouraged by dealers.

A similar coincidence of art-historical research, comparative availability and a lack of representation in major museums, particularly in Britain and North America, is shown by the very strong representation of Rubens, of whose work there are six major examples recorded in this book. A deep-rooted suspicion of this exuberant artist, based perhaps on the relics of the Puritan tradition, has meant that the great galleries of the UK and the USA have not inherited the rich holdings of his grand-scale compositions that their European counterparts have. The past decade has gone some way towards filling the gaps, notably with the *Gerbier Family*, published here in full for the first time, the *Samson and Delilah* purchased for the National Gallery in London, and the panel sketch for this picture now in Cincinnati. Rubens' greatest pupil, Van Dyck, never suffered from the same unpopularity. In particular the American taste, dating from before the First World War, for portraits from his Genoese period is shown to continue with the two contrasting examples illustrated here, the noble and imposing *Agosto Pallavicini* and the intimate and reflective *Portrait of a Genoese Nobleman*, both now in the USA. On the other hand the sketch entitled *Children of Charles I*, which featured on the catalogue cover of Agnew's 1968 exhibition of the artist, has happily stayed in this country. Rubens' other outstanding pupil, Jacob Jordaens, is however an art-historical rediscovery of the last fifteen years; few important works of his remain outside the old collections of Europe, and first-class examples such as the *Christ taken at Gethsemane* in the Cleveland Museum are now the subject of fierce competition.

Similarly the great names of the French seventeenth century, particularly the two expatriate artists Poussin and Claude, feature strongly, the diversity of the latter's work being shown in the span from the great *Judgement of Paris* in Washington to the small but jewel-like copper *Piping Herdsmen* in a private collection in Australia. Renewed interest in Claude's slightly older fellow-artist Elsheimer (again the subject of a major exhibition during the period) is represented by what is probably his masterpiece, *Il Contento*, in the National Gallery of Scotland. The mainstream of court-based French art is dominated by Largillière's portrait of the sculptor Nicolas Coustou, in which, as so often, the empathy of one artist for the talent of another has produced a likeness of outstanding immediacy and subtlety.

While it could be argued that it is the lack of availability of the great names of the Renaissance and the eighteenth century that has led to the new prominence of the seventeenth-century masters of Italy, Flanders and France, it must also be recognized that there has been a definite swing of fashion towards, and a development of taste for, the artists of this period. This is not true for the Dutch seventeenth-century artists, whose style and subject-matter has never really been out of fashion since their own time. The group recorded here is headed by the Rembrandt *Man in a Fur-lined Coat*, originally bought by Agnew's in 1927 for Governor Fuller of Massachusetts and sold in 1978 on behalf of the Fuller Foundation to the Toledo Museum of Art. The great names amongst the landscape artists are all represented – Van Goyen, the two Ruisdaels, Van de Capelle, Cuyp, Koeninck – while genre scenes by Steen and Ostade contrast with the clear light and ravishing detail of what must be one of Jan van der Heyden's greatest townscapes.

Part of the reason for the popularity of the Dutch seventeenth-century masters, particularly with private collectors, has always been their everyday subject-matter and their small scale, but a further important consideration has been their comparative availability. Private collectors are notoriously impatient people who like to buy in their chosen field as quickly as possible, and with the Dutch seventeenth century there are still many opportunities. Just the reverse is the case with the Spanish seventeenth-century painters. That only two appear in this record is a mark of their extreme scarcity, not their unpopularity. One of these, the Murillo portrait *Don Justino de Neve*, now strengthens the collection of the National Gallery in London in an area long recognized as one of its few comparative weaknesses, while the other, the Zurbaran *Birth of the Virgin*, is in California, a part of the USA with particularly strong Spanish connections in its early history.

English painting of the eighteenth and nineteenth centuries has long been a speciality of Agnew's, since the days when Thomas Agnew sold works by Bonington[2] and Turner in the lifetimes of the artists. The heyday of the English portrait in the grand manner was of course the 1920s, and after the experiences of slump and war had destroyed this, there was a reaction in the 'fifties and 'sixties against the society portraitists towards a more intimate and natural view of English life, with its conversation pieces, sporting pictures and landscapes. This led to a number of new English artists being elevated to the heights formerly commanded by Reynolds and Gainsborough: Zoffany for his conversation pieces, of which the *Cowper and Gore Families* must rank as one of the finest; Stubbs for his horses and exotic animals such as the cheetah; Wilson, Crome and Cotman for their individual views of the British landscape, which, whether based on Italian or Dutch precedents, founded a new and truly national tradition. But since 1967, while the new-found popularity of these artists has not changed, there has also been a revival of interest in the grand manner of English painting, partly as a result of a change of taste in Britain and the USA but particularly as the countries of continental Europe have at last begun to realize the importance of the British school within the European tradition. This revival has, however, centred on different aspects of the portraitists from the taste of the 'twenties, though pictures such as the *Villebois Children* by Gainsborough or the portrait *Paulet St John Mildmay* by Hoppner, that long-neglected artist, could easily have graced the collections of Huntington or Frick. There has been a new emphasis on the informal portrait, Reynolds' *Mrs Abington* sucking her thumb, – the reflective pose of the writer Lawrence Sterne, and Lawrence's 'picturesque' view of the inventor of that term, Payne Knight. Even Gainsborough has been valued most as a landscape artist or as the creator of the Romantic genre known as 'fancy pictures'.

Above all, it is the emergence of Turner, not only as the pre-eminent English artist but also as one of the great international figures of the nineteenth century, that has been the outstanding change of the period in question. A series of exhibitions, of which Agnew's 1967 show was the first, has been devoted to him, and the publication of a catalogue of his oil paintings (of which Evelyn Joll, one of Agnew's managing directors, was co-author) brought his name to even greater prominence. Since 1967 Agnew's have sold, amongst other oils, two of the few exhibited works by the artist still privately owned, *Ostend* and *Bonneville, Savoy*, and a major example of his late, almost abstract style, the *Val d'Aosta*, as well as large numbers of watercolours, of which *Longships Lighthouse* must be reckoned as the finest example of an English subject, while *Goldau* is pre-eminent amongst the late views of Switzerland.

As with Turner, other artists of Victorian England have received belated recognition from the continent of Europe as well as from the USA, and while much of this interest has been undiscriminating and fashionable in the worst sense (as many who had bought in the boom of the early 'seventies were to find in 1975), it has served to emphasize the importance of the Pre-Raphaelites themselves in contrast to their imitators. Of the next generation Burne-Jones, for so long the pet hate of the twentieth-century critic, has now been recognized as an important contributor to the European symbolist movement, a point well made by the presence of his series illustrating the Perseus legend in Germany, though one of his finest pictures, the *Laus Veneris*, has found a permanent home in England.

One field which has shown great increase in popularity over the period has been that of the Camden Town Group of British artists in the early years of this century. Once again, exhibitions and art-historical research have played a great part, and while the prices of the boom of the early 'seventies only gradually returned to these levels after 1975, and while as yet this school does not have an international reputation, it has definitely found a place in the hearts of many British private collectors. Sickert has for long been an Agnew favourite, but Gilman, represented in this record by one of his finest pictures, Gore and Bevan are comparative newcomers; so is Charles Conder, of special interest to Australian collectors because of his early career.

If the scarcity of objects of the highest quality has been one of the great features of the art market in the last fourteen years, in no field has this been more true than that of Old Master drawings. The difficulty in finding great works of the Renaissance is exaggerated by the fragile nature of works on paper, regarded as working drawings rather than as works of art and therefore often neglected or destroyed. Those that have survived from this period, such as the Fra Bartolommeo or Giulio Romano, are for this reason especially prized. From the eighteenth century finished drawings such as the Canaletto drawing from the Rosebery collection at Mentmore, originally intended as collectors' pieces, have been scarcely easier to find. A fine series of Fragonard drawings illustrating the story of Orlando Furioso, one of which appears here, forms a rare and beautiful set from France. As in the Old Master picture section, it is again the seventeenth century which provides the largest number of drawings: Annibale Carracci, Guercino, Rubens and Claude.

Scarcity has meant that many dealers have over the last few years broadened the range of objects in which they deal. For Agnew's this has meant the sale of a number of Persian miniatures from the 'Houghton *Shahnameh*', the finest illuminated manuscript of the great flowering of art that occurred under the Safavid dynasty. Three of these miniatures are reproduced here. Islamic art has been the subject of a great deal of art-historical interest in recent years, mainly in the West where so many of its treasures were brought during the nineteenth century. The influx of oil money into their countries of origin led to a great boom in their popularity as collectors competed to bring back these lost treasures. Recent political events have however depressed this market, which was only just beginning to show signs of a broader international base.

In looking for new areas in which the purchase of high-quality objects and a broad range of attractive works is still possible, Agnew's has recently turned to sculpture and works of art. The first results of this new speciality appear in this record, together with the splendid enamel armilla from the coronation vestment of the Emperor Frederick Barbarossa bought at the von Hirsch sale for the Germanisches National-museum, Nuremberg. The final destination of our most important purchase in this field to date, the Algardi bust *Monsignor Antonio Cerri*, is still undecided.

One field in which Agnew's has increased its activities, but which does not appear in this record, is that of prints. During the late 'sixties, when looking for new areas of print-making into which to expand a stock based mainly on English and French eighteenth- and nineteenth-century prints, it seemed that fine impressions of the traditionally accepted Old Masters Durer and Rembrandt were almost impossible to obtain except as isolated examples. Opportunities did seem still to exist, however, in two fields: that of Venetian eighteenth-century etchings by Tiepolo, Canaletto and their contemporaries and in the great flowering of colour lithography at the end of the nineteenth century in Paris. Agnew's has held important exhibitions covering these areas and has bought and sold a complete set of Canaletto etchings and three important series of colour lithographs, Bonnard's *Quelques aspects de la vie de Paris*, Vuillard's *Paysages et Intérieurs* and on two occasions Toulouse-Lautrec's *Elles* series. Another field which has become a particular speciality is that of Whistler's etchings, where one collector is in the process of bringing together a complete group of the rare and beautiful Venetian subjects. The relative availability of good-quality prints in these areas and their not exorbitant price-range makes them attractive to museums and private collectors alike, and there can be no doubt that the print market will continue to expand and develop.

Half of this record is concerned with the search for new works of art in traditional fields, or for new fields to fit into a traditional framework; the other half is concerned with the owners, traditional or new, who have been found for them. But before analysing the pattern of ownership, it may be interesting to enquire where these works of art came from. Many of them were bought at auction, many for Agnew's own stock, some on behalf of museums and other clients (the latter works include, amongst those already mentioned, the Parmigianino *Portrait of a Collector* and the Tiepolo ceiling *Venus Entrusting Eros to Chronos* for the National Gallery in London, the Stubbs *Cheetah with Indians* for the Manchester City Art Gallery and Monet's *La Terrasse à St Adresse* for the Metropolitan Museum, New York). Some of these were already famous pictures when they appeared in the sale-room; others, such as the Gerard David, the Baldung and the Titian, were previously unknown. Many have come to Agnew's privately, some from collectors throughout the world who had bought, or whose families had bought, the pictures from Agnew's in the past, thus continuing a long personal connection, others from new clients who sought advice and help in disposing of their works of art. Many have come to Britain and then gone abroad again: the Gentile da Fabriano from Paris to Los Angeles, the Sassetta from continental Europe to Australia, the Largillière from Paris to Berlin, the Gentileschi from Florence to Cambridge, Massachusetts. Many of the Persian miniatures from the Houghton *Shahnameh* have travelled from Iran to Istanbul, on to Paris, then to New York and back to Europe. Such movements have of course long been part of the history of collecting, as the tide of history and material wealth has ebbed and flowed, and London since 1945 has been the entrepôt for such transfers. One significant movement can however be deduced from this pattern since 1967. Now that the collecting of European works of art has been a habit in the USA for several generations, an increasingly large number of such works are being sold and are finding their way back across the Atlantic as taste and styles of living change. Some of these, such as the pair of Veronese *Allegories of Navigation*, have crossed the ocean not once but twice, moving from one seaboard of the USA via a London auction and Agnew's to the other, as has also the Constable *Salisbury Cathedral* which left the USA for Agnew's and then returned to Canada. Others, notably Turner's *Ostend*, have passed from the USA to continental Europe, while the Gainsborough *Villebois Children*, bought in England by Lord Duveen in 1923, has returned from the descendants of the then purchaser to an English private collection.

It has for long been a cliché to point out that the great treasures of England are being pillaged by foreign collectors and museums. It is not nearly so often mentioned that the enormous concentration of high-quality works of art in Britain is the result not only of the absence of foreign invasion but of the pillaging of the continent of Europe by English collectors in the eighteenth and nineteenth centuries. An unfortunate note of hysteria often enters discussion of what has come to be called in the last decade the 'national heritage', and the definition of what is or is not part of it has gradually been widened as the movement for its protection has been identified with the broader movement for conservation in general. Naturally a country with limited wealth and important social priorities has had to ration the amount of money it can make available for museum acquisitions, but none the less, if this book can be taken as representative of a larger whole, the museums of the UK have an enviable record in the works they have acquired since 1967.

Nor is it only the National Gallery in London, whose acquisitions through Agnew's have already been mentioned, that has taken the opportunity of enriching its collection. Edinburgh has continued its post-war tradition of selective purchasing of great pictures by adding from Agnew's Crome's *The Beaters* and the Seurat landscape, in addition to the Ruskin Madonna, the Elsheimer and the late Guido Reni. To Cardiff has gone the Cima from the Loyd collection; to Liverpool the Montagna from the Merton collection (surely one of the most enchanting small pictures known by this rare artist); the National Portrait Gallery has bought the Reynolds Sterne, the Barber Institute in Birmingham the Bassano and the Sickert *Eldorado*, Leicester the Sweerts, the Manchester City Art Gallery the Gainsborough *Faggot-gatherer* as well as the Stubbs, and the Laing Art Galley (Newcastle-upon-Tyne) the Burne-Jones. Lastly, the Victoria and Albert Museum has purchased the ivory bust *Hamlet Winstanley*, the firm's first sale to a national museum in the field of sculpture. Many other museums in this country have made purchases from Agnew's not included in this record and it has always been the firm's policy to offer whenever possible any object of potential interest to museums in Britain before selling to clients abroad.

If the UK museums have had, in the form of central and local government aid, at least some support in the face of inflation, the English private collector, whose importance as the means of replenishing the national heritage is so often forgotten, has not. During the expansionary phase of the early 1970s many new collectors emerged, particularly in the fields of English eighteenth- and nineteenth-century painting. But the depression of 1974–5 eliminated some, and in the second half of the decade sharply rising prices and the sharply falling value of the pound swept away most of the rest. Of the ones who remained, those with the necessary means concentrated on the traditional fields of Dutch and English painting, but most were compelled to adjust their tastes to their pockets and confine their activities to English water-colours, to British twentieth-century painting, and to prints, where foreign competition was not so strong and prices were therefore more reasonable. It is a sad comment on Britain's relative economic, and hence collecting, power that on average under 10 per cent of Agnew's turnover since 1974 has resulted from purchases by private UK collectors.

Outside the UK, the greatest clients of Agnew's, and indeed of all fine art dealers, must be in the North American continent, for nowhere else is found that peculiar relationship of public institution and private patron on which so much of its capacity to collect depends. The pattern of public responsibility and private patronage is a complex and changing one. Many of the east-coast museums, founded many years ago and enriched by the gifts or bequests of numerous public-spirited trustees, have had to undergo a major change as the concept of a public institution privately controlled by donor trustees has had to be replaced by a greater measure of public accountability. In many of these the accent has changed from acquisition to presentation, and funds which formerly would have been devoted to purchases have had to be used to cover the inflated costs of rebuilding and running the institutions. None the less, Agnew's old clients, especially the Metropolitan in New York and the National Gallery in Washington, have made important purchases in the period, notably in the fields of seventeenth- and eighteenth-century Italian, French and Flemish paintings, as well as drawings from the same periods – all areas which donors of a previous era had tended to neglect.

In the mid-west, Toledo and Cleveland have continued to add to their choice collections. Toledo has taken the Lorenzo Monaco, the Guido Reni *Venus and Cupid*, a rediscovered masterpiece of the artist's maturity, the Rembrandt and the early Poussin *Holy Family* (which came to Agnew's from the stock of a London picture-framer who had bought it for the frame rather than the canvas): a discerning and imaginative selection which is a great tribute to the eye and judgement of the museum's former director. To Cleveland have gone the delicate Neroccio *Madonna and Child* and the robust Goya from the Contini collection in Italy, as well as the Jordaens.

But the most notable development in the museum world in the USA since 1967 has been the emergence of the Los Angeles museums as powerful acquirers. Over the period the Los Angeles County Museum has been transformed by the acquisition of a major group of High Renaissance paintings, through the generosity of the Ahmanson Foundation: the Fra Bartolommeo *Madonna and Child*, also from the Contini collection, the re-discovered Titian portrait *Giacomo Dolfin*, recorded by

Vasari but unknown since leaving the collection of the sculptor Canova in 1820, and the two full-length Veroneses, not to mention the last and most poetic of the three Guido Renis that Agnew's have handled in recent years. Meanwhile a few miles away, the giant but still slumbering Getty Museum has begun slowly to stretch its immense muscles. To the nucleus of a collection left to it by Mr Getty, including the Van Dyck portrait *Agosto Pallavicini*, have been added from Agnew's the *Portrait of a Man*, attributed by some to Francia but by others to Raphael himself, and the superb Gentile da Fabriano *Coronation of the Virgin*, arguably the most beautiful and important picture to pass through Agnew's in the period of this record. A few miles to the east by a typically American transformation, a private collection has become a museum, as the Norton Simon collection has been installed in the Pasadena museum. The Old Master section of this collection has been put together only in the last twenty years, long after many people would have believed that such a thing was possible, and as such it is an amazing achievement. Since 1967 Agnew's has supplied the early Guercino *Cleopatra*, Rubens' *Three Marys at the Sepulchre*, from the artist's most classical period (formerly in the Czernin collection in Vienna), and the Zurbaran *Birth of the Virgin*.

If California has been the new home for so many Old Master paintings in the 'seventies, Texas may be just that for the 'eighties, the purchase by the Kimbell Art Museum, Fort Worth, of Annibale Carracci's *Butcher's Shop*, one of the first realist subjects to be painted by an Italian artist and a seminal work of baroque art, being perhaps a forerunner.

On the east coast, another major transformation from private collection to public museum occurred in April 1977 with the foundation of the Yale Center for British Art and the gift to it of a major part of Mr Paul Mellon's collection of British paintings. Though parts of this collection had been frequently exhibited in Britain and the USA, to see the display in the new Yale building showed everyone how in a few years a collection of British art had been assembled to rival the best that Britain itself could show. The English section of this record contains many fine paintings and watercolours which are now at Yale or are expected to go there, amongst them Reynolds' *Mrs Abington*, the superb Wilson of *Dinas Bran*, the Zoffany, the Turner of *Bonneville* and one of the greatest of the American artist Copley's portraits of his English period, *Master Richard Heber*.

Another name that occurs frequently in the English painting section of this record is that of the Bayerische Staatsgemäldesammlungen, Munich. As has been said, it is only in the last few years that continental museums and collectors have begun to realize the importance of British art, but even if they have come late to the field they have entered it with enthusiasm and perception. Munich has accumulated a group of major British paintings, headed by their Turner and including a glowing Wilson (*The Thames at Richmond*), and a late Gainsborough landscape once in the collection of George IV. In Germany also the Kunsthalle in Hamburg has been buying English paintings, while the Louvre in Paris and the Rijksmuseum in Amsterdam have been acquiring their first examples of watercolours and drawings in this school. Though three of Berlin's purchases from Agnew's have been in the Old Master field, the Moroni *Duke of Albuquerque* from Warwick Castle and the Guercino *Madonna and Child*, a most beautiful example of the artist's early style, as well as the Largillière portrait, it has also bought a major British portrait, Gainsborough's *Joshua Grigby*. Of other German museums which are Agnew's clients, Stuttgart specializes in Italian eighteenth-century paintings, including the Amigoni portrait of the celebrated castrato singer Farinelli, while its sister museum Karlsruhe has added an early Pater.

The museums of the old Commonwealth have long been clients of Agnew's. Since 1967 the National Gallery of Canada has added three diverse pictures of high quality to its collection, the Baldung published here by the gallery's former director, the Poussin modello for the artist's first major commission, the altarpiece of *The Martyrdom of St Erasmus*, in St Peter's, Rome, and the full-size Constable sketch *Salisbury Cathedral*. Agnew's contacts with Australia also date back many years, but these have been transformed recently as the result of a series of exhibitions which the firm has held in that country since 1971. Two great pictures have gone to the National Gallery of Victoria, the Sassetta predella panel from the *Arte della lana* altarpiece, painted by the artist in 1423–6 for the wool guild of Siena, and the Turner *Val D'Aosta*, which for many years previously had been in the Groult collection in Paris. The new Australian National Gallery has bought prints and sculpture from Agnew's, and the other state museums have acquired a variety of paintings. But the major discovery of the exhibitions held in Australia has been the readiness of the Australian public to interest themselves in European works of art. As a result two private collectors have in the last decade put together outstanding groups of paintings, many of which are illustrated here.

If this introduction has had to concern itself more with museums than private collectors, that is one of the penalties of attempting to write contemporary history when discretion must be reckoned as a cardinal virtue. All the same, the evidence of this record shows how vigorous the collecting urge still is amongst individuals, and it must be recognized as one of the most rewarding parts of an art dealer's life to see taste change with experience and collections grow with perception. As has been said, this has not been an easy period for the English collector. Nor has the habit of collecting privately on the Continent ever really recovered from the ravages of the war. It is therefore in America that the greatest private collectors are to be found, often closely related to and taking advice from museums, but still exercising their basic and inalienable right of personal choice. Since 1967 a considerable change in taste has developed in American private collecting. At that time, the fashion was all for the impressionists, with only a very few collectors looking towards the Old Masters. Gradually a taste for the 'easier' schools of Flemish and Dutch painting evolved amongst a much wider buying public and many of those who started their collection in this area have now 'progressed' towards a much more catholic interest throughout the field of Old Master painting. An unstable dollar has encouraged those previously uninterested in the arts to enter the market for economic as well as commercial reasons; England's lesson of the early 'seventies has now been learnt by the USA.

However many generalizations can be made from this record in showing changes of taste and fashion in the art market, it is none the less a personal record of one London firm. A family business is only as strong as the interest of the family in it, and it is good to record that over the period two more great-great-great-grandsons of Thomas Agnew have joined the business while another has become a non-executive director. A business can only last as long as the loyalty of its employees, and in 1975 one more name was added to the list of people employed by the company for over fifty years. It is only as good as the friendship it earns from its business associates, and while the sad death of Rudolf Heinemann in 1975 deprived Agnew's of one of its oldest friends, it has in the period gained a new one in Eugene Thaw. A company's tradition is only as important as its readiness to change, and in the last few years a major transformation of the Bond Street gallery, itself a hundred years old in 1976, has taken place, by means of modernization and repairs that are partly visible, partly invisible, to the ordinary visitor. And in 1973 the services to the arts of Geoffrey Agnew, the dominant figure in the history of this family business in the post-war period, were recognized by the award of a knighthood.

As for the future, no doubt the next decade will have as many problems as the last fourteen years. But Agnew's hopes that the tradition of dealing in the finest-quality works of art will, despite this, be maintained and that a future publication will record as large and varied a selection of these as does this book.

---

[1] *Agnew's 1817–1967*, Geoffrey Agnew, published privately in 1967.

[2] Bonington's *The Grand Canal* still bears a label showing it was sold by Thomas Agnew before 1828.

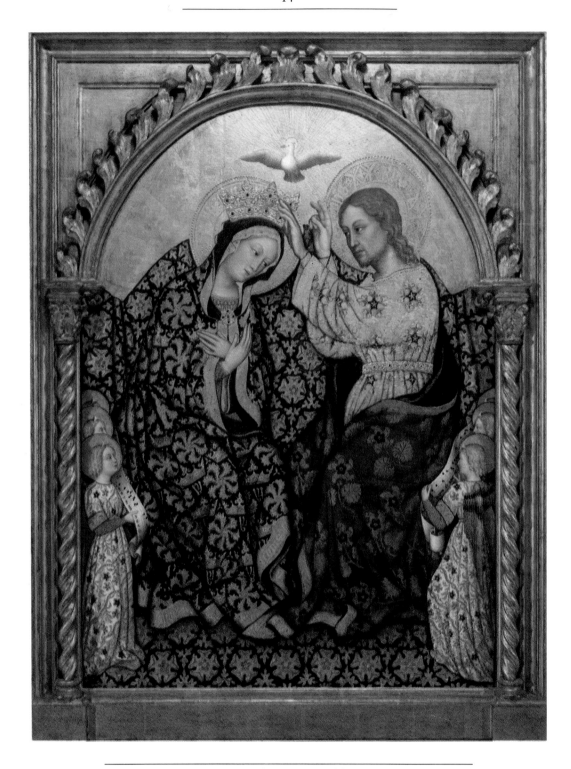

Figure 1 Gentile da Fabriano, *The Coronation of the Virgin*, 36¹⁄₂×25 inches,
The J. Paul Getty Museum, Malibu, California, 1976

Gentile's
Coronation of the Virgin

KEITH CHRISTIANSEN

The purchase of the *Coronation of the Virgin* by Gentile da Fabriano has brought the Getty Museum one of the few remaining privately owned paintings by a major fifteenth-century Italian artist. It shows the Virgin and Christ seated at opposing angles on a brocade-covered throne, the sides of which define a shallow space in front of the gold background (fig. 1). Six angels, disposed three to either side, mark off the foreground and hold scrolls inscribed with musical notations and the words from the fifth chapter of the book of *Revelation: Timete dominum et date illi hono[rem]/Dignus est agnus qui o[ccisus est]*. Cleaning in 1977 has revealed the painting to be in good condition. The most serious losses are in the glazes which once modelled the brocade behind the figures and the sleeve of Christ's garment. The raised gilt ornament, known as *pastiglia*, is largely modern, though already present in a water-colour reproduction of the painting made in the 1830s.[1] Though the panel has been thinned, cradled and cut down, the picture surface has not been cropped, and the outlines of the enframing capitals are still visible below the springing of the arch.

Until 1835, when the Reverend John Sanford bought the painting in Florence, it was in Gentile's hometown of Fabriano, about ninety kilometres north-east of Perugia. There, in 1827, the local artist Vincenzo Liberati described it as follows:

Two easel paintings [by Gentile] exist in this our venerable seminary, one showing the Coronation of the Virgin and the other Saint Francis receiving the stigmata; they are on a gold ground and of excellent facture; they were ceded as a gift by the Franciscans to the Filippins, and now, these being suppressed, are in the possession of the seminary.[2]

Another hand cryptically added in the margin: 'quindi venduti' – since sold.

The *Stigmatization of St Francis* has long been identified with the beautiful painting now in a private collection in Parma (fig. 2), but which remained until about 1923 in the Fornari collection in Fabriano, where it was seen by Sir Charles Eastlake in 1858. It shows St Francis kneeling before a grove of small oak trees, above which the peak of Mount La Verna rises. Across a narrow ravine stands a small Romanesque chapel, in front of which is portrayed brother Leo shielding his eyes against the brilliant seraphic appearance of Christ. The scene is remarkably close to the description of the event found in the fourteenth-century *Fioretti*. The painting is in excellent condition; its panel has been thinned, cradled, and cut in almost identical fashion to the *Coronation*. The two paintings have equal dimensions and the traces of the enframing capitals on the *St Francis* exactly match those on the *Coronation*, suggesting that the two are a pair.

This hypothesis is supported not only by the provenance of the two paintings but also by the references to a copy of both compositions made by several authors well into the nineteenth century. Once again Liberati, who attributed these copies – probably correctly – to the local fifteenth-century artist Antonio da Fabriano, is the earliest source. More interesting is the fact, noted by Cavalcaselle, that on the chapel depicted in the *Stigmatization of St Francis* was the inscription AÑO DÑI 1452 DIE 25 DE MARTIO – twenty-five years after Gentile's death, and that when seen by Passavant in 1835, the two paintings formed a double-sided processional standard. The copies are last mentioned in Fabriano in 1873. The *St Francis* may be traced until 1892, and the *Coronation* is almost certainly to be identified with that given by Prince Johann von Liechtenstein to the Gemälde Galerie in Vienna in 1882.

An idea of the paintings' original appearance is provided by a

Figure 2 Gentile da Fabriano, *Stigmatization of St Francis*,
Private Collection, Italy

Figure 3 Gentile da Fabriano, *Adoration of the Magi*, Uffizi, Florence

processional standard in the Galleria Nazionale at Perugia, also by a Fabrianese artist, showing on one side the Madonna and Child, and on the other the Annunciation. The Getty and Parma paintings must have formed a similar standard: a rectangular damage at the base of each panel would thus be the result of a common mount by which they could be carried on a pole. The figure of God the Father, conspicuously missing from the *Coronation,* probably appeared in the tympanum above. The fact that both paintings formed a single ensemble casts strong doubt on the current notion that they date from two long-separated phases in Gentile's career and underlines the confusion that still mars an understanding of his development.[3]

The two touchstones of Gentile's career are the altarpieces of the *Coronation of the Virgin* in the Brera in Milan (fig. 4) and the *Adoration of the Magi* in the Uffizi in Florence (fig. 3). The first is generally dated about 1400.[4] However, since it was evidently painted for the high altar of Santa Maria di Valdisasso near Fabriano, where Flavio Biondo saw it towards the middle of the century, it cannot have been begun before 1406, when the

ruined buildings were purchased by Chiavello Chiavelli for the Observant Franciscans. It had probably been commissioned by 1412, when Chiavello died, and was finished before 1414, when Gentile moved to Brescia where he was continuously active until September 1419. The *Adoration of the Magi* was painted for the sacristy of Santa Trinità in Florence. It is dated 1423, but was probably underway by November 1422, when Gentile is listed in the painters' guild in Florence as living in the quarter of S. Trinità.

In the Brera *Coronation of the Virgin,* isolated passages of carefully observed flora enliven an essentially abstract and decorative image, the underlying constructional principle of which is an involuted curve repeated in each of the several panels. The entire repertory of the medieval craftsman's technique is used to create an incomparably varied surface, as in the tongues of flames emanating from the Christ and the Virgin. The effect is both rich and languid. The surface of the *Adoration of the Magi* is still richly embellished, especially in the costumes of the kings and the trappings of the horses, but the emphasis has shifted. The figures are more acutely rendered and stand more solidly. The stylized hills or small enclosed gardens in the pinnacle scenes of the earlier altarpiece have been transformed into full-blown landscapes with distant vistas of incredible variety, and, in the predella scenes, atmospheric skies. A new and far-reaching naturalism has re-shaped the pictorial content. The Getty-Parma standard clearly associates itself with this later phase. By comparison to the Brera *Coronation*, the figures are modelled with greater strength, their faces less generalized, and the drapery falls in heavier folds that relate more functionally to the underlying forms. In place of the heavenly splendour of tooled rays in the central panel of the polyptych is found the regal setting of an earthly throne, and in contrast to the schematic landscape of the pinnacles, there is the carefully described peak of Mount La Verna enlivened by a light emanating from the seraphic figure of Christ. A consequence of that light is what are probably the first consistently projected cast shadows in Italian painting since the Lorenzetti brothers.

The figures in the main scene of the *Adoration* offer the closest parallels to those in the *Stigmatization of St Francis*, while the Moses and David, who recline on the central arch in the tympanum, and the blessing Christ in the rondel have much in common with the more hieratically conceived and richly garbed figures of the *Coronation*. This close relationship with the *Adoration of the Magi* allows a relatively secure dating for the standard: certainly it cannot post-date the *Adoration*, for in subsequent paintings like the small altarpiece in the Frick Collection, New York, or the panels of the Quaratesi altarpiece, once signed and dated 1425, Gentile shows a greater mystery of sculptural form and a preference for paler colours combined with oil glazes of deep wines and olive greens.[5] Given its provenance from a Franciscan church in Fabriano, there is, in fact, every reason to believe that the standard was commissioned in March or April 1420, when Gentile made a request to Tommaso Chiavelli, Lord of Fabriano, for exemption from taxes, 'that he might live and die and practise his trade in Fabriano'. Significantly, the request was granted. When the devotion of Tommaso's father, Chiavello, to the Franciscans is recalled – not only did he purchase S. Maria di Valdisasso for the Observants, he was also buried within its walls – one is even tempted to conjecture that Tommaso was the patron.

If the Getty-Parma standard was the result of a commission in a provincial centre of central Italy, its iconography none the less links it with Tuscan art. Only in Tuscany, and above all in Florence, is there a tradition for depicting Christ simultaneously crowning and blessing the Virgin. The earliest extant example of this rare iconography occurs in a late thirteenth-century mosaic on the inside façade of the cathedral of Florence,

Figure 4 Gentile da Fabriano, *Coronation of the Virgin*, Pinacoteca di Brera, Milan

where music-making angels already appear at the sides. It was apparently revived at precisely the moment Gentile painted the processional standard. In a purse made for the Medicis' friend, the anti-Pope John XXIII, a reversal of the cartoon has resulted in Christ blessing with his left hand, but the basic elements of the scene are unchanged. The significance of this depiction remains problematic, but its singularity leaves little doubt that Gentile must have been familiar with these or similar examples. In the light of this, it is not surprising that the style of the Getty *Coronation* also seems indebted to earlier Florentine painting. An image very like Jacopo di Cione's *Coronation of the Virgin* in the National Gallery in London (no. 569) seems to have served as a model both for the general placement of the figures and their presentation in front of a brocade cloth of honour.

When we ask ourselves why Gentile should have been interested in an image some fifty years old while Lorenzo Monaco's more fashionable and recent *Coronation of the Virgin*, now in the Uffizi, apparently passed unnoticed, the answer must be that only in the Cione could Gentile find solidly constructed figures combined with a wealth of surface ornamentation. Few facts are more significant than this repudiation of the hard, swinging forms of Florentine International Gothic, but Gentile shared this choice with the young Masaccio, whose earliest altarpiece from S. Giovenale in Cascia, dated 1422, is strictly Cionesque in the rigid presentation of its figures modelled in carefully defined planes. However, comparison of the Getty *Coronation* with Masaccio's altarpiece underlines the greater subtlety of Gentile's painting and confirms what can also be deduced from the succession of outstanding commissions that fell to him in Florence: prior to about 1424 he was the predominant painter in Italy.

The Florentine elements in the Getty painting constitute the surest proof that Gentile had taken up residence in Florence before 1422. Indeed, when Gentile left Brescia in late September 1419, it was to join Pope Martin V, who was then residing in Florence. It therefore seems quite possible that Gentile stopped in the city before journeying to Fabriano the following year. This hypothetical stop-over would perhaps most readily explain the Florentine traits of the *Coronation*. It would also explain why several Florentine paintings completed about the same time as the *Adoration of the Magi* already evidence a familiarity with works by Gentile that would otherwise be difficult to account for. In his *Annunciation* in S. Trinità, Lorenzo Monaco, who is documented only to 1423, has interpreted the scene more rationally and naturalistically than in any of his earlier works. And in the *Madonna and Child* at Bremen, dated 1423, Masolino makes his debut as a direct follower of Gentile:

the touching intimacy of the figures, their soft chiaroscural modelling, and such details as the ringlets of the Child's hair allude to a painting very like Gentile's *Madonna and Child* in the National Gallery in Washington, which seems to pre-date the Getty *Coronation* and may be Gentile's earliest Florentine commission.

Both for its aesthetic qualities and the probable circumstances surrounding its conception, the Getty *Coronation of the Virgin* lends new understanding to Gentile's enigmatic career. It also underlines, by comparison, the precocity of the *Stigmatization of St Francis*, for whatever the beauties of the *Coronation,* the *St Francis* is the more revolutionary work. In the profound naturalism which infuses the details of the landscape and informs the system of lighting; in the almost archaeological objectivity by which Gentile has created a Romanesque chapel ornamented on the exterior with a Dugento mosaic of the Annunciation and on the interior with a Dugento altarpiece, a challenge was made to a whole generation of younger artists. Only one, Masaccio, understood the full implications of this new kind of image that based itself on a study of nature. In turn he so out-distanced Gentile that for 500 years the latter has been remembered, if at all, as the most beautiful flower of Italian Gothic painting.

---

[1] B. Nicolson, 'The Sanford Collection', *Burlington Magazine*, XCVII, 1955, p. 210, discusses the water-colour copies of paintings purchased by John Sanford. A photograph of the one after the Getty painting is on file in the German Institute in Florence.

[2] 'Due quadri da cavalletto esistono presso questo nostro V. Seminario, raffiguranti l'uno la Coronazione di M. V. e l'altro S. Francesco che riceve le stimate; questi sono in fondo d'oro d'un lavoro eccellente; tali quadri furono ceduti in dono dai PP. Francescani ai Filippini, ed ora, soppressi questi, sono passati in dominio de V. Seminario.' See B. Molajoli, *Gentile da Fabriano*, Tip. Gentile, Fabriano, 1927, p. 112, note 2.

[3] All of Gentile's paintings with a provenance from Fabriano – with the exception of the Getty *Coronation* – have traditionally been dated early in his career, but even a superficial glance at these works – the *Madonna and Child with Saints* in Berlin-Dahlem, the altarpiece in the Brera, and the Parma *St Francis* – shows this idea to be untenable. E. Micheletti, *L'opera completa di Gentile da Fabriano*, Rizzoli, Milan, 1976, cat. nos. 1, 2–11, 12 & 22 gives the most recent summary. R. Longhi, 'Me pinxit: un San Michele Arcangelo di Gentile da Fabriano', *Pinacotheca*, I, 1928, pp. 71 ff., first suggested that the Getty painting was the centre of a polyptych with a Saint Michael, now in the Museum of Fine Arts, Boston, as a flanking element. Micheletti, *op. cit.*, cat. nos. 22–5, has revived this argument, but without foundation. The St Michael measures 99.6 × 37.4 cm against the 87.5 × 64 cm of the *Coronation*, its format is different, and it is not by Gentile. Equally unfounded is the notion of L. Grassi, *Tutta la pittura di Gentile da Fabriano*, Rizzoli, Milan, 1953, p. 60, that the picture surface of the *Getty Coronation* has been cropped and originally included God the Father directly above the dove.

[4] See E. Micheletti, *op. cit.*, cat. nos. 2–11.

[5] The Quaratesi altarpiece is now divided between the Uffizi, the Royal Collection, Windsor, the Vatican, and the National Gallery, Washington.

20

Nardo di Cione, *The Virgin and Child*, 27¼×17 inches, Private Collection, Switzerland, 1969

Lorenzo Monaco, *Madonna and Child*, 48½×24 inches,
The Toledo Museum of Art, Gift of
Edward Drummond Libbey, 1976

Stefano di Giovanni, called Sassetta, *A Miracle of the Sacrament*,
9½×15 inches, National Gallery of Victoria, Melbourne,
purchased with the aid of a State Government Grant, 1976

Neroccio di Landi, *The Madonna and Child*, 18¼×12
inches, The Cleveland Museum of Art, Purchase,
Leonard C. Hanna Jr. Bequest, 1980

Sano di Pietro, *St Donatus and the Dragon*, 8½×14¼ inches, Private
Collection, England, 1967

Figure 5 Verrocchio, *Ruskin Madonna* after cleaning and restoration in 1973–5. Canvas transferred from wood, 42×30 inches, National Gallery of Scotland, Edinburgh

Verrocchio's
Ruskin Madonna

HUGH BRIGSTOCKE

When John Ruskin, in 1877, paid £100 for a fifteenth-century Florentine picture of the Madonna (fig. 5), kneeling in adoration of the infant Christ, and set against an imposing background of ancient Roman ruins, he hailed it enthusiastically as 'an entirely priceless example of excellent painting, exemplary for all time'. This judgement was endorsed when the National Gallery of Scotland, supported by the National Art Collections Fund and the Pilgrim Trust, acquired the picture for its permanent collection from the Trustees of the Guild of St George in 1975, the negotiation being handled by Agnew's. Yet this masterpiece of Renaissance painting, which Ruskin's friend and agent Charles Fairfax Murray had attributed to Andrea del Verrocchio but which nevertheless quickly became associated instead with the name of its first British owner, had not always enjoyed such warm critical admiration. In the Manfrini collection, Venice, where Ruskin and Fairfax Murray first found it, it lay neglected and apparently ruined. We have this on the authority of another distinguished English critic, Charles Eastlake, who had already seen the picture twice during the 1850s but made no effort to acquire it. In 1855 he dismissed it brusquely as 'ruined . . . perhaps P. Uccello'. Two years later, striking a more positive note, he recorded: 'Madonna adoring Child on ground – much injured (Child's legs) but formerly careful specimen and might be restored . . . architecture and background very carefully executed. Called Lippi . . . probably Pesello.'

By the time Ruskin was in a position to ship the picture home to England, the paint surface was flaking so badly that a transfer to canvas from the original wooden support was prescribed as an immediate necessity. Only then was the picture allowed to make the journey to its new owner, St George's Museum at Walkley. Yet to Ruskin, at least, it seemed exactly the right picture on which to found his Sheffield School of Art.

Sadly the picture's past neglect continued to exact its toll, and in 1892, just after it had been moved to Ruskin's new museum at Meersbrook Park, Sheffield, the condition of the paint surface was again causing concern, the gesso ground having become detached from the canvas in some areas. According to William White, the museum's curator, the 'only remedy . . . was the delicate operation of entirely removing the *gesso* itself, which was cautiously planed away, until the back of the paint first laid on was exposed'. After this second transfer within the space of only fifteen years, no further restoration work is recorded until 1973 when the Trustees of the Guild of St George sent the picture to John Brealey in London for the removal of the by now badly darkened and discoloured nineteenth-century varnish and the extensive overpainting which together almost totally obscured the quality of the original paint surface. Following Brealey's meticulous and sensitive work we are now at last in a position to make an objective assessment of the picture's condition. To judge from the evidence of paint losses along what were clearly the lines of the old joins in the panel, we can see that the original support consisted of three planks lying vertically. The right-hand plank apparently retained less of the pigment than the other two, so that the condition of the paint surface to the right of a line through the Madonna's left shoulder is noticeably worse than elsewhere. Such damage has left the essential structure of the design unimpaired. The heads and hands are also relatively intact. The least well preserved areas are the Child's legs and the Madonna's drapery in the lower right corner.

Notwithstanding its damaged condition, the *Ruskin Madonna,* which must date from *c.* 1470, represents the epitome of the aspirations and internal contradictions of the early Florentine Renaissance. This is true of both its design and its icono-

Figure 6 X-ray detail of the *Ruskin Madonna*, reproduced by permission of the Courtauld Institute, London

graphy. An X-ray of the picture, made at the Courtauld Institute, London in 1960 (fig. 6), reveals an elaborate network of perspective lines, incised in the gesso with a sharp stylus, with the diagonals converging on a point just below the Madonna's hands. This perspective grid (much of which can also be detected with the naked eye) appears to have been worked out directly on a panel prepared in the usual manner, rather than transferred from a separate cartoon. This almost didactic emphasis on linear perspective, combined with an entirely traditional technique, was an essential element of fifteenth-century Florentine Renaissance art, which had already been mastered and ably demonstrated by artists such as Uccello (to whom

Eastlake had tentatively attributed the Ruskin picture), and which was then further developed and exploited by the talented artists in Verrocchio's workshop. Vasari describes Verrocchio himself as an expert in perspective, and this is confirmed by study of the artist's relief of the *Beheading of St John the Baptist* on the Silver Altar now in the Cathedral Museum, Florence, as well as the foreground of the Pistoia altarpiece (commissioned from Verrocchio in 1479 and completed with help from assistants, principally Lorenzo di Credi, *c.*1485). We find a similar preoccupation with elaborate perspective construction in an early work of Verrocchio's most illustrious pupil: Leonardo da Vinci's celebrated drawing of the *Adoration of the Magi* in the Uffizi. And as Everett Fahy has observed, Domenico Ghirlandaio, another artist to come under Verrocchio's influence, although not apparently a member of his studio, also matches the perspective of the Ruskin picture in his documented early fresco (1476) of the *Last Supper* at Passignano.

In iconography too Ruskin's picture strikes a delicate balance between traditional Christian subject-matter and a new self-conscious respect for the legacy of the classical world. Everett Fahy, in a remarkably stimulating public lecture (commissioned by the National Gallery of Scotland to celebrate the picture's acquisition) has shown that the picture represents the Adoration of the Child *alla antica*. The ruins shown in the background are the remains of the Temple of Peace, a Roman basilica that was supposed to have collapsed the night Christ was born, according to a tradition recorded *c.*1275 in the *Golden Legend* of Jacopus de Voragine, Archbishop of Genoa. Throughout the Middle Ages and the Renaissance the Temple of Peace was identified with the Basilica of Constantine in the Forum in Rome. Fahy believes the ruins shown in the *Ruskin Madonna* evoke the basilica sufficiently to suggest that the Florentine artist had some accurate information about the building's appearance.

Yet the *Ruskin Madonna* offers far more than an artistic synthesis of the mathematical and classical discoveries which we associate with the Florentine Renaissance. It is remarkable above all for its marked individuality, the inimitable delicacy of its execution, especially the luminous silvery tone which invests the Madonna with an aura of divinity, a beauty far transcending mere physical grace. Even the architecture, so impressive in the simplicity of its design, signifies much more than an antiquarian's literal reconstruction of an antique ruin; as it recedes into the far distance, pointing towards a landscape beyond our reach, it evokes a haunting atmosphere of mystery which was to mesmerize the imagination of Bernard Berenson, and awake in him a romantic sense of nostalgia for an irrecoverable past. '*Correndo con lo sguardo oltre il disegno del pavimento e le vuote basi fino ai pilastri, gemmei nell' eleganza dell' intaglio, fino alle mure dalle delicate commettiture, e al di là dell' arco a lacunari fino alle basse colline sull' orizzonte lontano, io sono stato sopraffatto, come di rado m' è avvenuto nella mia lunga esperienza estetica, da un romantico desiderio che nulla ridesta tanto fortemente quanto le nobili tracce dell' antichità classica.'* ('And looking across the patterned pavement over empty bases for pillars, gem-like in elegance of carving, to walls of daintily jointed masonry, and through a coffered arch to the low hills on the distant horizon, I am overcome as but seldom in my long aesthetic experience by a romantic yearning for the far-away and long-ago, which noble vestiges of classical antiquity so unfailingly arouse.')

Berenson then went on to discuss the picture's attribution. He followed Fairfax Murray in attributing not only the construction and design but also much of the execution, including the architecture, to Verrocchio. *'Sarebbe facile pensare a Leon Battista Alberti come creatore di quello sfondo architettonico, eppure il Verrocchio l'ha dipinto.'*

Yet Berenson must have realized that there is no fully authenticated picture by Verrocchio which in any way approaches the manner in which the Ruskin Madonna is executed. The picture's essential link with Verrocchio is in the perspective construction and the design, and Berenson's attribution should be regarded as a purely speculative option, a response to his recognition of the picture's exceptional quality and central art-historical significance. If we turn now to Verrocchio's autograph paintings, the figure of S. John the Baptist in the Uffizi *Baptism of Christ* (a picture commissioned for the monastery of San Salvi and completed by Verrocchio with assistance from Leonardo da Vinci, according to Vasari) or the *Madonna and Child* in West Berlin (Inv. 104), which although undocumented is widely accepted as by the same hand as the S. John in the Uffizi picture, we become conscious of qualities very different from the rigid linear outlines and silvery, even lighting of the *Ruskin Madonna*; instead we have a robust strength in the modelling of the figures, a fine precision in the rendering of details, combined with a remarkably fluent line of sensitive contours, and above all a subtle use of chiaroscuro which throws the forms into light relief.

It is in response to these observations that some recent writers have begun to look beyond Verrocchio for the author of the *Ruskin Madonna*, although this would not necessarily preclude Verrocchio's responsibility for the original concept. Alberto Martini's attribution to the young Leonardo da Vinci was made in 1960 before the picture was cleaned and has attracted no fresh support. His argument was in any case based more on the picture's perspective construction than on the style of execution. More interest surrounds the idea, independently advanced

Figure 7 Detail from the *Ruskin Madonna* after cleaning in 1973–5

by Federico Zeri (in a letter of 9 September 1976) and Everett Fahy since the picture was cleaned, and subsequently followed by Sheldon Grossman, that it might be by Domenico Ghirlandaio. According to Vasari, Domenico Ghirlandaio was a pupil of Alesso Baldovinetti, but to judge from works such as the documented fresco *Madonna of Mercy*, from the Vespucci chapel in the church of Ognissanti, Florence, he was also closely influenced by Verrocchio around 1470. Fahy argues that in Domenico Ghirlandaio's work alone do we find an exact parallel for the meticulous handling of paint, the handsome physical types, the exceptionally static design, the doctrinal projection of space and the interest in antiquity which characterize the *Ruskin Madonna*. Further, he indicates that the pilasters in the background of the *Ruskin Madonna* can be seen in Ghirlandaio's early frescoes at Brozzi, Cercina and Passignano, as well as in his *Adoration of the Shepherds* in S. Trinità, Florence; while counterparts for the barrel vault are to be found in Ghirlandaio's frescoes in S. Maria Novella, Florence.

Fahy also associates the *Ruskin Madonna* with a small group of undocumented pictures, all representing the Virgin and Child, and all apparently dating from *c*.1470. Of these, one (fig. 8) is in the Louvre, Paris (Inv. 1367A); it was first attributed to Domenico Ghirlandaio by Berenson in 1933. Another is in the National Gallery of Art, Washington (Inv. 1412), where it is attributed to Domenico Ghirlandaio on the authority of Zeri. A third, from the monastery at Camaldoli, only recently rediscovered, bears a traditional attribution to Domenico Ghirlandaio which received further support in 1974–5 when it was exhibited under this name at Arezzo. Grossman, who had earlier suggested it might be by Verrocchio, has also now accepted the attribution to Domenico Ghirlandaio.

Although the arguments advanced by Fahy for attributing the *Ruskin Madonna* to Domenico Ghirlandaio deserve considerable respect, I nevertheless elected to place the picture under the name of Verrocchio and workshop in my critical catalogue of the *Italian and Spanish Paintings in the National Gallery of Scotland* (1978). A museum catalogue must of necessity adopt a conservative approach to new attributions (if only to avoid constant changes and consequent administrative chaos!), and I took the view, which I still maintain, that the onus of proof lies with Zeri, Fahy and others who would attribute the picture to Domenico Ghirlandaio. It is still a little difficult to believe that such a young and immature artist, about twenty years old in 1470, was capable of achieving its delicate luminous tonality and the mysterious quality of the architectural background. One does not even find these distinctive qualities in Domenico Ghirlandaio's mature work; but of course artists do not necessarily improve with age and success. At the same time I enthusiastically endorsed Fahy's brilliant insight that the *Ruskin Madonna* might be by the same hand as the three undocumented paintings described above. I was particularly impressed by the links between the Ruskin picture and the picture in the Louvre. The Washington picture (now disfigured by what appears to be a modern gold background) is arguably more prosaic in spirit – the figures, although animated in gesture, somewhat heavy and wooden in execution, the use of light less sensitive and delicate; its stylistic connection with the *Ruskin Madonna* is perhaps less clear-cut. Nevertheless the facial features of the Washington Madonna are exceptionally close to the Madonna in the Ruskin picture, and it is easy enough to appreciate the basis for the view of the picture advanced by Fahy. As for the Camaldoli picture, I have never seen it; but Ulrich Middeldorf has independently advanced the view (in letters of 21 January 1976 and 28 September 1977) that it is by the same hand as the *Ruskin Madonna*. He differs from Fahy only in the belief that both pictures are by Verrocchio.

Since the publication of the Edinburgh Catalogue, Konrad Oberhuber has published a stimulating but highly controversial

Figure 8 Domenico Ghirlandaio (attributed), *Virgin and Child*, Louvre, Paris

article on the stylistic development of Verrocchio, in which he too accepts the stylistic proximity of the Ruskin picture and the picture in the Louvre. He attributes both to Verrocchio, but then complicates, and arguably confuses, the issue by adding to the same group further Verrocchiesque works which, in the opinion of most previous writers, are by a wide variety of different hands: a *Virgin and Child* in Frankfurt which Zeri has attributed to the Master of the Gardner Annunciation and which Grossman has recently associated with Domenico Ghirlandaio; a *Virgin and Child with Angels* in the National Gallery, London (Inv. 296), and a closely related picture in West Berlin

Figure 9 The *Ruskin Madonna* before cleaning and restoration in 1973–5

mainly on undocumented works such as the *Ruskin Madonna* which provide no secure basis from which to advance.

At this juncture it may perhaps be more useful to isolate and underline one small area of general agreement, amidst all the conflicting views on the authorship of the Ruskin picture. This is the clear stylistic link with the *Virgin and Child* in the Louvre. If no firm attribution for the *Ruskin Madonna* and the picture in the Louvre can be substantiated – and we still await the publication of Fahy's researches and deliberations on Domenico Ghirlandaio – we may be obliged to take refuge in the old-fashioned art-historical device of inventing a portfolio name for this elusive but highly individual artist. It seems strangely paradoxical that the picture now in Edinburgh, universally acknowledged as a masterpiece of the Florentine Renaissance, should even today be saved from anonymity only by virtue of its association with the name of the eminent collector and critic who rescued it from almost certain destruction and total oblivion just over one hundred years ago.

BIBLIOGRAPHY

Charles Eastlake, *Notebooks* (National Gallery, London MSS) 1855, II f.6 v. and f.9 v; 1857 III f.1 r.

William White, *The Principles of Art as illustrated by examples in the Ruskin Museum,* London, 1895, p. 74.

John Ruskin, *The Works of John Ruskin,* Library Edition ed. E. Cook and A. Wedderburn, London, 1907, XXX p. 193.

Bernard Berenson, *Verrocchio e Leonardo, Leonardo e Credi* in Bollettino d'arte XXVII, 1933, pp. 193 ff and pp. 241 ff.

Bernard Berenson, *The Drawings of the Florentine Painters,* Chicago, 1938, I p. 53.

Federico Zeri, *Il Maestro dell'Annunciazione Gardner* in Bollettino d'arte XXXVIII, 1953, pp. 125 ff.

Alberto Martini, *Ipotesi Leonardesca per la 'Madonna' Ruskin* in Arte Figurativa: antica e moderna VIII, 1960, pp. 32 ff.

Martin Davies, *National Gallery Catalogues, The Earlier Italian Schools,* London, 1961, pp. 553 ff, inv. no. 296.

Sheldon Grossman, *The Madonna and Child with a Pomegranate and Some New Paintings from the Circle of Verrocchio* in Report and Studies in the History of Art 1968, National Gallery of Art, Washington, II, 1969, pp. 47 ff.

[Anna Maetzke], *Arte nell'Aretino* Exhibition Catalogue, San Francesco, Arezzo, 1974, pp. 100 ff, no. 37.

Everett Fahy, *Ruskin's Verrocchio Madonna in Edinburgh,* unpublished public lecture, commissioned by Edinburgh, 26 October 1976.

Hugh Brigstocke, *Italian and Spanish Paintings in the National Gallery of Scotland* Edinburgh, 1978, pp. 186 ff, inv. no. 2338.

Konrad Oberhuber, *Le problème des premières oeuvres de Verrocchio* in Revue de l'Art 42, 1978, pp. 63 ff.

Sheldon Grossman, *Ghirlandaio's Madonna and Child in Frankfurt, and Leonardo's Beginnings as a Painter* in Stadel Jahrbuch 7, 1979, pp. 101 ff.

Fern Rusk Shapley, *Catalogue of the Italian Paintings, National Gallery of Art, Washington* I, 1979, p. 205 no. 1412.

(Inv. 108) which are both often described as Umbrian, although Grossman has advanced the possibility of Botticelli; and an altarpiece in Budapest, already attributed to Verrocchio by Vasari, but more generally attributed since to Biagio d'Antonio.

Oberhuber's attribution of the *Ruskin Madonna* (and other works) to Verrocchio is not therefore to be seen as a conservative posture, adopted as a defence against the still unsubstantiated attribution to Domenico Ghirlandaio propounded by Zeri and Fahy. It requires a total reorientation of our views on Verrocchio as an artistic personality and on the organization of his workshop. Yet it depends, perhaps to an alarming extent,

Andrea del Sarto, *Madonna and Child*, 32¼×26 inches, William A. Coolidge
Collection, Cambridge, Massachusetts, 1971

Baccio della Porta, called Fra Bartolommeo, *The Holy Family*,
60×36½ inches, Los Angeles County Museum of Art,
Gift of the Ahmanson Foundation, 1973

Attributed to Francesco Francia, *Young Man in Red*, 26½×21 inches.
The J. Paul Getty Museum, Malibu, California, 1976

Cima da Conegliano, *The Virgin and Child*, 23¹⁄₂ × 18¹⁄₄ inches, National
Museum of Wales, Cardiff, 1977

Bartolommeo Montagna, *Madonna and Child*, 15×14 inches, Walker Art
Gallery, Liverpool, 1978

Giovanni Battista Moroni, *The Duke of Alburquerque*, 44×33 inches,
Staatliche Museen Preussicher Kulturbesitz Gemäldegalerie Berlin (West),
1979

Girolamo Francesco Maria Mazzola, called Parmigianino, *A Collector*,
35×25¼ inches, purchased on behalf of the Trustees of the
National Gallery, The National Gallery, London, 1977

Tiziano Vecelli, called Titian, *Giacomo Dolfin*, 40½×35¼ inches, Los
Angeles County Museum of Art, Gift of the Ahmanson Foundation, 1980

Jacopo Robusti, called Tintoretto, *Portrait of a Young Man as David*,
48×39 inches, National Museum of Western Art, Tokyo, 1972

Paolo Caliari, called Veronese, *Allegory of Navigation with an Astrolabe*,
81×46 inches, Los Angeles County Museum of Art,
Gift of the Ahmanson Foundation, 1974

Paolo Caliari, called Veronese, *Allegory of Navigation with a Cross Staff*,
81×46 inches, Los Angeles County Museum of Art,
Gift of the Ahmanson Foundation, 1974

Domenico Zampieri, called Domenichino, *Landscape with Moses and the Burning Bush*, 17¾×13¼ inches, Mr and Mrs Charles Wrightsman, 1970, by whom presented to the Metropolitan Museum of Art, New York

Jacopo da Ponte, called Jacopo Bassano, *Adoration of the Magi*, 37×51 inches, The Barber Institute of Fine Arts, Birmingham University, 1978

Annibale Carracci, *The Coronation of the Virgin*, 46½×56 inches, The Metropolitan Museum of
Art, New York, Purchase Bequest of Miss Adelaide Milton de Groot (1876–1967), and Dr and
Mrs Manuel Porter and sons, gift in honour of Mrs Sarah Porter, 1971

Annibale Carracci, *The Butcher's Shop*, 23¹⁄₂×28¹⁄₄ inches,
Kimbell Museum, Fort Worth, 1980

Giovanni Francesco Barbieri, called Il Guercino, *Cleopatra*, 46×37 inches, Norton Simon Foundation, 1973

Giovanni Francesco Barbieri, called Il Guercino, *The Mystic Marriage of St Catherine*, 34⅝×27½ inches, Staatliche Museen Preussicher Kulturbesitz Gemäldegalerie Berlin (West), 1970

Figure 10 Orazio Gentileschi, *Madonna with the Sleeping Christ Child*, 39⅛×33½ inches, The Fogg Art Museum, Harvard University. Given through William A. Coolidge in memory of Lady Marian Bateman, 1976

Gentileschi's
Madonna with the Sleeping Christ Child

SYDNEY FREEDBERG

Formerly in the Contini-Bonacossi collection in Florence, Orazio Gentileschi's *Madonna with the Sleeping Christ Child* (fig. 10) has come to the Fogg Art Museum at Harvard University, given through Mr William A. Coolidge in memory of Lady Marian Bateman. The picture has no known provenance prior to its ownership by the famous Italian dealer, who acquired it from an unspecified private collection in Milan. In 1931, when the painting was still in this Milanese collection, it was published for the first time, with the correct attribution to Orazio Gentileschi, by Amadore Porcella in his catalogue of the Galleria Spada.[1] Roberto Longhi affirmed the attribution in the context of his article of 1935 on the French Caravaggists,[2] and in 1943[3] he attempted to establish a documentation for the picture, connecting it with letters of 1609 and 1610 from Rome to Mantua describing a Madonna painted by Orazio for the Duke Vincenzo. The painting to which these letters refer, however, cannot possibly be our *Madonna with the Sleeping Christ Child*; it is different in every respect save that of the 'Madonna' subject and the colour.[4] Our picture has appeared on subsequent occasions in the literature, always with full assent to the attribution to Orazio.[5]

Though the painter's chronology has not so far been precisely ordered,[6] this painting's place within Orazio's *œuvre* is, even in a quite close sense, as certain as the attribution. We have seen that Longhi's association with the letters of 1609 and 1610 was incorrect, but the time of origin must none the less have been quite close to this. The permissible latitude of dating would be no earlier than *c*.1610 and not later than *c*.1615; the earlier term is the much more likely one. It is to the *David in Contemplation* of the Galleria Spada (fig. 11) that our painting, despite the disparity in subject-matter, shows a truly pressing analogy; and while Longhi's case for the dating he proposed for

the *David, c*.1610–11, is not objectively provable it is most widely accepted in the literature.[7] There is in the two pictures an almost interchangeable effect of generosity of form and richness of surface, a resembling quality of movement in the body, and a comparable state of mind, linked with the quality of movement. Substance, surface and emotion in the two pictures proceed from one inspiration. To another painting – or, more precisely, set of paintings on a common theme, of *Judith and Holofernes* – which has more objective ground than the *David* to be assigned to the same moment, *c*.1611, the Fogg *Madonna* offers likenesses in almost the same degree. The Hartford version of the *Judith* theme (fig. 12) may come the closest in its breadth and textured density of forms, in their quality of interacting posture and emotion, and in their salience from a darkened ground. Actually documented in 1611 and early 1612, the recently recovered frescoes with a *Concert of Female Figures* in the Casino delle Muse of the Palazzo Pallavicini-Rospigliosi offer further likenesses.[8] All these works, the Fogg painting included, stand in a special and commonly identifiable stage in Orazio's evolution; they have emerged from the preceding phase, thinner and more facetted in form and more complicated in lighting – more dependent upon the recent Caravaggio – into a new fullness, indeed a monumentality, of shape and scale, and a new power and consistency of light. A little later, towards 1615, this breadth in conception and in execution would, in most instances, be invaded by an increasing concern with the particular – with finer and more specified effects of form and lighting, most evidently in the draperies. The ex-Liechtenstein *Girl with a Lute* (Washington, National Gallery) (fig. 13) otherwise so close in quality and appearance to the *Madonna with the Sleeping Christ Child,* is already incipiently so touched.[9]

Figure 11 Orazio Gentileschi, *David in Contemplation*, Galleria Spada, Rome

ferent in date, typify this phase. But with the Fogg *Madonna* and its chronological companions Orazio passed beyond dependence on the art of Caravaggio into a powerful and highly personal style, for which the prior assimilation of Caravaggism was a threshold. There is, in the Fogg *Madonna*, a sudden growth to grandeur in the conception of the form and theme, an absolute command of the image into unity, and a strength and integrity of feeling that is in a different reach from the emotions in the preceding pictures. The Fogg picture exemplifies this new style at its first and most expansive moment. It conveys a near-illusion of living flesh and sumptuous drapery, revealed by a pure and brilliant light; the colour too – blond flesh tones relieved against the cerulean blue of the Madonna's mantle and the radiant, peculiarly Gentileschian, golden-yellow of her dress – is light-saturated. Unlike the pictures of the preceding phase, this work has no part of Caravaggio's tenebrism. It is a blond painting, but in this blondness, and in the purity of lighting and large form that accompany it, it still resembles Caravaggio – not the Caravaggio of recent years but the youthful master of the old century's last decade, when Gentileschi must first have encountered his art and been magnetized by its novelty. This lucidity of colour, light and shape at the same time recalls the Tuscan Mannerist tradition: there is an admitted look to the Fogg painting as of a Bronzino remade in the modern vocabulary.[10] Too much can be made of this resemblance, however; it must be recalled that, while Orazio was born a Tuscan, and insisted on his Florentine inheritance, it was his ancestry, but neither his birth nor his upbringing that was Florentine, and his experience of the high Maniera style of Florence could hardly have been significant. His own earlier career as a Maniera painter was in a style that quite overlooked the precedents of Bronzino or any Florentine analogue of his. The example of a blond and lucid style that was present to Orazio in Rome, and more immediate in its power to influence his art, was certainly the early Caravaggio's. A further element in Orazio's style, in particular as he affirms it in this moment, suggests a relationship with Maniera precedent that also may be illusory: his graphic definition of silhouette and the fine-etched precision he employs in passages of detail; but these, again, are in the early Caravaggio.

Orazio's deviation from Caravaggio's example has been in an intensification of an aspect of what is loosely called Caravaggio's 'realism': in the adaptation of Caravaggesque light not only to the purpose of the affirmation of presences but to the use of them as resonators and reflectors of the light, affirming beyond effects of presence a verging on illusion. Orazio's light makes lucent brilliance of the blond-toned flesh, and probes the surfaces of drapery to make textures of a richness for which

The pictures of this phase in general, and the Fogg *Madonna* in particular, represent a critical moment in Orazio Gentileschi's career. Already by this time in his later forties, Orazio had been converted less than a decade before from the practice of an unremarkable, even tedious, late Maniera style to a sensitive and personal interpretation of the contemporary demonstrations of Caravaggio – with Giovanni Baglione, whose allegiance to Caravaggio was tentative, short-lived, and far less comprehending, the earliest instance of a substantive response to Caravaggio's revolutionary example. From a time that must not much precede 1605 through the rest of the decade Gentileschi assimilated and mastered the essentials of the style of thought, as well as the tools of style, of Caravaggio's art, but with an effect of delicacy in form and emotion that were foreign to the exemplar: the *Baptism of Christ* (Rome, S. M. della Pace, *c*.1605) or the *Ecstasy of St Francis* (Rome, Galleria Corsini), not much dif-

Figure 12 Orazio Gentileschi, *Judith and Holofernes,* Wadsworth Atheneum, Hartford, Connecticut

Caravaggio's own art showed no precedent. This is not just a deviation from Caravaggio's persistently classicizing model, but in a sense a development beyond it, towards a quality of baroqueness, and it is an invention in the history of seventeenth-century painting style.[11] It anticipates, and must in some measure have been an inspiration for what the Caravaggists of French and Netherlandish origin, merging old native inclination with a modern Italian mode, would make a preoccupation of their art in close succeeding years.

Capitalizing on his invention, Orazio in the Fogg *Madonna* and its contemporary works has made a painting in which a large part of the formal and expressive burden is carried by the drapery, magnified in its extent and in life of movement, light and colour given to it to become an aesthetic and expressive agent equal with the human actors. The intensity and brilliance with which this resource has been exploited create illusion, but the illusionism is but one effect among a battery of ideas and sensations that the drapery conveys: among them a sense of majesty in its amplitude and sweep and of precious splendour in its luxury and colour that are appropriate to garb the Queen of Heaven and to enframe her Child. Later in his long career, Orazio would often be the supreme tailor in paint that Longhi describes,[12] but here his intention reaches far above mimetic skill or fine visual sensation towards a region that makes analogue in its colour and its luministic force with the painting of the youthful Titian. Behind the devices of his art, however, there is a grandeur in Orazio's conception of his theme that gives his image its effect of a dimension that expands in the spectator's experience of it beyond the limits of its frame.

The image combines majesty with seeming truth of actual existence, and grandeur with the closeness and particularity of a scene of genre. Beneath the modernity of Caravaggesque stamp

Figure 13 Orazio Gentileschi, *The Lute Player*, National Gallery of Art, Washington

that conveys the effects of reality and genre there is a set of traditional religious references of deep seriousness. The naked Child sleeps on the white sheet as on a shroud, prefiguring His sacrificial death.[13] The Virgin, recalling a motif made famous by Raphael in the *Madonna del Velo* once in S. M. del Popolo,[14] lifts her veil over Him. Commonly, the veil also may denote the shroud, but since the white cloth beneath Christ is here so explicit in its sense, it is likely that the veil intends a separate meaning. It is of course a traditional symbol of mourning, appropriate to this context; but it also calls to mind the custom of ancient Roman religion that required the celebrant at a sacrifice to be veiled, and in turn the rôle in the Christian Mass of the humeral veil which covers the vessels of the Eucharistic sacrifice.[15] In His left hand the sleeping Child holds a fruit which ordinary experience would lead us to expect to be the apple of Original Sin, but which is not that nor the less frequent attribute of the peach, pear, or pomegranate. The fruit has been identified exactly as an apricot,[16] for the presence of which in this context I have found no precedent or contemporary example. It would appear that we are dealing in this instance with a quite exceptional – and sophisticated – case of Biblical textual criticism. The fruit of the Tree of Knowledge most likely could not have been an apple. Moldenke[17] summarizes the long controversy about the identity of the Biblical fruit, of which the species proposed besides the apple include the orange, citron, pomegranate, quince, fig, grape and apricot. Only the last, Moldenke concludes after a careful review of the evidence, seems to meet all the specifications of the Biblical references. This conclusion was a frequently published one in nineteenth-century writing on the problem, but I have not been able to find the source which, *c*.1610, supplied to Orazio Gentileschi the special and arcane knowledge that the apricot, not the apple, should have

been the true fruit of Original Sin, which Christ's sacrifice meant to redeem. But it is clear, *prima facie*, that this learned substitution was what was intended, and the fruit in Jesus's hand supplies the motive and necessity for the sacrifice the theme foretells. It is conveyed, finally, that the whole image is, as it were, a transubstantiation into their real presences, here made splendidly visible, of the elements of the Eucharist: the body of Christ, in a sleep that foretells His offering in sacrifice, is revealed beneath the humeral veil upon His shroud, the cloth laid on an altar which is the broad lap of Mary Virgin, who is Mother Church. The image is as eloquent in symbol as it is in substance, a point of rare ascent in Gentileschi's art.

---

[1] A. Porcella: *Le pitture della Galleria Spada*, Rome, 1931, pp. 5–6.

[2] R. Longhi: 'I pittori della realtà in Francia ovvero i caravaggeschi francesi del seicento', *L'Italia letteraria*, XI, no. 3, 19 January 1935, p. 5, fig. 27. Captioned illustration only, without discussion in text.

[3] 'Ultimi studi sul Caravaggio e la sua cerchia', *Proporzioni*, I [1943], pp. 22, 46 n. 36.

[4] The painting for Mantua is described in some detail in the letter of 24 October 1609 written by one Bartolommeo Pellini to G. Magno, Secretary of the Duke Vincenzo; published with the letter of 13 February 1610, also from Pellini to Magno in A. Luzio: *La galleria dei Gonzaga venduta all'Inghilterra nel 1627–1628*, Milan, 1913, pp. 60–1. The points of difference against the Fogg picture emerge quite clearly from the text of the letter of 1609:
... *Il Gentileschi m'incomincia a riuscire in fatti, poiché 4 di sono mi venne ad invitare ch'io andassi a vedere il quadro che fa ad istanza di V.S., il quale si trova quasi in totale perfettione, et per mio poco giuditio sarà cosa molto rara et degna certo di ogni gran Principe. È una Madonna a sedere con il bambino in braccio, nudo da un poco di fascia in poi che le copre un pochino il corpo, che cinti et ambi duoi si guardano con affetto grand.*[mo] *con tutto ch'il bambino sia d'età d'un mese et non più, ma ben fatto et natural.*[te] *La Madonna è vestita di giallo con un manto azzurro, che se bene le cade per terra fa però bella vista et ornam.*[to] *È di bell.*[ma] *faccia senza alcun ornamento di capo fuor che la diademma, et ha le spalle scoperte et nude, onde si vede il bello fatto dalla natura. Nè altro mi spiace in esso quadro se non l'essere assai picciolo, perchè non sarà a pena, nè se bene mi raccordo, credo siano 4 palmi d'altezza et 3 di larghezza, per il che malam.*[te] *ci capisce la figura per essere de buona statura, et piutosto grossa che mediocre. Insomma si conosce che il naturale è bonis*[ma] *robba.*

[5] A. Emiliani: 'Orazio Gentileschi: nuove proposte per il viaggio marchigiano', *Paragone*, IX, 1958, p. 42. H. Wethey: *El Greco and His School*, Princeton, 1962, Vol. II, p. 59. M. Rosci: *Orazio Gentileschi*, Milan, 1965 (unpaginated). R. Bissell: *The Baroque Painter Orazio Gentileschi, His Career in Italy*, doctoral thesis presented at University of Michigan, 1966 (University Microfilms), Vol. II, pp. 128–33, this last the fullest and most reliable discussion so far not only of the present picture but of the larger subject.

[6] The closest definition of Orazio's chronology in Bissell, *op. cit.*, with which compare the earlier work, on Gentileschi's Marchigian paintings, by Emiliani, *op. cit.*, pp. 38–57. The basic, and still partly valid, indications of a chronology are those of Longhi in the article in *Proporzioni* cited in note 3 above.

[7] Longhi's proposition ('Gentileschi, Padre e Figilia', *L'Arte*, XIX, 1916, pp. 270–1) is that the landscape is a collaboration by Agostino Tassi, who returned to Rome in 1610, and with whom Orazio broke by early 1612, when Agostino was tried for the alleged rape of Artemisia Gentileschi. H. Voss:

Malerei des Barock in Rom, Berlin, 1925, pp. 45–9; Emiliani, *op. cit.*, pp. 42–3; F. Zeri: *La Galleria Spada in Roma*, Florence, 1954, pp. 86–7; R. Buscaroli: *La pittura di paesaggio in Italia*, Bologna, 1935, p. 328, accept Longhi's proposition and resultant dating.

[8] See H. Hibbard: 'Scipione Borghese's Garden Palace in the Quirinal', *Journal of the Society of Architectural Historians*, 23, 1964, pp. 164–5 and F. Zeri: 'The Pallavicini Palace and Gallery in Rome, I: The Palace', *Connoisseur*, CXXXVI, 1955, pp. 184–8.
I am not including among the comparative items the *St Jerome* painting, in 1943 in a Milanese private collection, which was attributed to Gentileschi by Longhi, *op. cit.*, 1943, p. 22, fig. 40, and associated on evidence from the Tassi trial with a time of origin in 1611. My exclusion is because I can draw no certain conclusions as to Gentileschi's authorship from Longhi's published photo. It should be noted, however, that Bissell, *op. cit.*, Vol. II, pp. 93–5, is inclined to regard the attribution to Gentileschi as correct.

[9] Bissell, *op. cit.*, Vol. II, pp. 133–8, also considers the Washington picture of a slightly later date, within the same general timespan, than the Fogg *Madonna*. He articulates the difference between them thus: '... the increased fluidity in the application of the highlights and the greater airiness to the whole are signs of a slightly later phase in the period of 1610 to 1615.'

[10] Longhi, *op. cit.*, 1943, p. 22: '*quasi un Bronzino fattosi caravaggesco.*'

[11] It should not be discounted that not only Elsheimer and Saraceni but also the youthful Rubens move in a similar direction before the end of the first decade, but the effects in them that are similar are far less intense than in Gentileschi.

[12] As for example in Longhi, *op. cit.*, 1916, p. 272.

[13] Cf. G. Firestone: 'The Sleeping Christ Child in the Renaissance', *Marsyas*, II, 1942, pp. 43–62.

[14] Raphael did not invent the motif: see Firestone, *op. cit.*, for earlier instances. The small Raphael School piece, the *Madonna with the Sleeping Christ Child and St John*, in the Louvre, is another instance of the theme. The most famous intervening example between those by Raphael and our Gentileschi is Sebastiano del Piombo's in the Museo di Capodimonte, Naples.

[15] Cf. in *Encyclopedia Italiana*, ed. 1937, vol. 35, pp. 32–3 and bibliography thereto.

[16] I am very grateful to Dr Richard A. Howard, Arnold Professor of Botany and Professor of Dendrology, Director of the Arnold Arboretum, for help in this identification and for references to the botanical literature.

[17] H. N. Moldenke and A. L. Moldenke: *Plants of the Bible*, Waltham, 1952, pp. 184–8, 286–7 note 167.

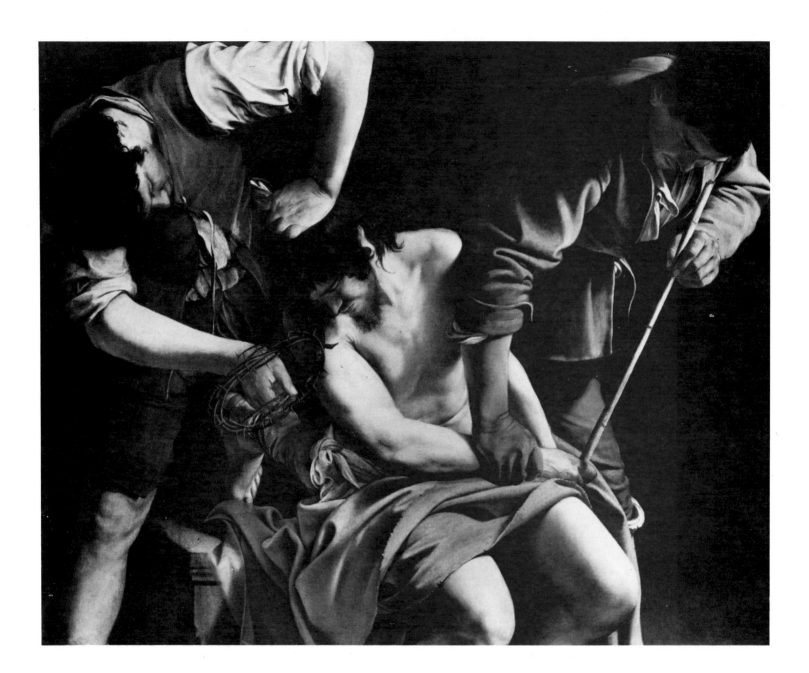

Orazio Gentileschi, *The Crowning with Thorns*, 47×58½ inches,
Herzog Anton Ulrich-Museum, Braunschweig, 1977

Guido Reni, *Bacchus and Ariadne*, 38⅝×34 inches, Los Angeles County
Museum of Art, Gift of the Ahmanson Foundation, 1978

Guido Reni, *Venus and Cupid*, 90×61 inches, The Toledo Museum of Art,
Gift of Edward Drummond Libbey, 1972

Guido Reni, *Moses and Pharaoh's Crown*, 53×68 inches,
The National Gallery of Scotland, Edinburgh, 1979

Giovanni Battista Tiepolo, *Venus Entrusting Eros to Chronos*,
115×75 inches, purchased on behalf of the Trustees of the National Gallery,
The National Gallery, London, 1969

Giovanni Battista Tiepolo, *The Martyrdom of St Agatha*,
19¾×11⅝ inches, The Home House Trustees, 1969

Jacopo Amigoni, *Carlo Broschi called Il Farinelli*, 49×41 inches,
Staatsgalerie, Stuttgart, 1972

Gaetano Gandolfi, *A Lute Player*, 30×22½ inches,
Private Collection, UK, 1967

Giovanni Antonio Canal, called Il Canaletto, *A View on the River at Padua*,
20¼×33 inches, Private Collection, USA, 1974

Giovanni Antonio Canal, called Il Canaletto, *Warwick Castle: the South Front*,
28½×47½ inches, Private Collection, USA, 1980

Francesco Guardi, *Grand Canal, Venice*, 19¹/₂×30 inches,
Private Collection, USA, 1973

Francesco Guardi, *Church of San Cristoforo di Murano*,
18¾×30 inches, Private Collection, USA, 1973

Giovanni Paolo Panini, *The Interior of St Peter's, Rome*, 61×77½ inches,
National Gallery of Art, Washington, Ailsa Mellon Bruce Fund, 1968

Figure 14 Hans Baldung Grün, *Eve, the Serpent and Death*, 28¼×12¾
inches, The National Gallery of Canada, Ottawa, 1972

Baldung's
Eve, the Serpent and Death

JEAN SUTHERLAND BOGGS

It is not only that Eve in *Eve, the Serpent and Death* (fig. 14) by Hans Baldung Grün is quite consciously a seductress; the small painting is in itself a seductive work. At the National Gallery of Canada in Ottawa we began to succumb to its sorcery when in 1969 we heard stories from Sotheby's about a picture formerly attributed to School of Cranach which an Edinburgh schoolmistress had wanted to sell and which had been reattributed in the sale-rooms to Hans Baldung Grün. It was then sold on 3 December of that year to Thomas Agnew for the considerable sum of £224,000. The story of the discovery of a masterpiece in an auction house was in itself a provocation to see the work. But in addition it had a substantial pedigree. The schoolmistress's grandfather, from whom she had inherited it through an uncle, had been the estate agent of the Duke of Devonshire. In addition, it had been sold at Christie's in 1875 as Lucas Cranach from the collection of William Angerstein, whose grandfather, John Julius Angerstein, had formed the collection that is the nucleus of the National Gallery, London. It therefore had the romance of associations at least with the names of two of Britain's greatest collectors. And in Ottawa it had another appeal, even from that distance. We had good German Renaissance pictures but nothing by Baldung and nothing with as provocative a subject as *Eve, the Serpent and Death*. Consequently, the reputation growing around the work acted as a magnet to draw us across the Atlantic.

Myron Laskin, Jr, our Research Curator of European Art and roving explorer for works of art, went to London first where he saw the painting before Sotheby's sold it and, obviously, before Agnew was able to have it cleaned. He was enthusiastic but somewhat overawed by the eventual price – more than the National Gallery of Canada had, up to that time, ever paid for a work of art. In the meantime Gyde V. Shepherd, the resident Curator of European Art, would not let us forget the painting's attractions. As a result, I went to see it in 1971, completely succumbed to the work's beauty, and returned with the determination that the National Gallery of Canada should buy it, which it did in 1972. For a series, *Masterpieces in the National Gallery of Canada* edited by Dr Laskin, Professor Robert A. Koch of Princeton University published the work in a short monograph; I recommend his perceptive explanation of the painting to anyone reading this.

In justifying the acquisition of the work, which I had to do to the Visiting Commitee of the National Gallery of Canada, the Board of Trustees of the National Museums of Canada, and the Treasury Board, I naturally emphasized its significance for our small but fine collection of German Renaissance art. Ottawa has a lyrical *Madonna of the Flowering Pea* that is close to Lochner and four sixteenth-century portraits, two by Bartel Bruyn, two by Bartel Beham. One of the male portraits by Beham has what is probably its original frame, inlaid with engraved ivory and studded with amber. The other is, however, an infinitely more subtle work, the sophisticated portrait of an effete prince, which had been bought through Agnew from Prince Liechtenstein. There are two paintings attributed to Cranach: a *Christ and the Adulteress*, a robust work from the early part of his career, and a large painting of an attenuated Venus, which was once owned by Marshal Goering. None of these works can, however, in itself express the intellectual and religious complexities of Reformation Germany in the way that the Baldung does. None of them brings the religious and secular together in such a telling relationship. None has quite the same intensity as a work of art. And none could be described as a miniature masterpiece.

Ottawa has three other paintings which could help to put the Baldung in its context in the Northern Renaissance. One is a

Figure 15 Hans Memling, *The Virgin and Child with Saint Anthony Abbot and a Donor*, 36½×21⅛ inches, The National Gallery of Canada, Ottawa

Virgin and Child with St Anthony Abbot and a Donor (fig. 15) of 1472 by Hans Memling who had been born and trained in Germany but had left it for Flanders some seven years before. Another is a *Crucifixion* which Quentin Matsys painted with strong Catholic fervour in Antwerp not long after Baldung painted *Eve, the Serpent and Death*. (Both were bought from Prince Liechtenstein through Agnew.) The third is a painting within a painting. In a *Portrait of Lady Dacre* by Hans Eworth, there is a portrait of her late husband by Hans Holbein, representing a younger generation of German painters than Cranach and Baldung.

Behind my conviction that this Baldung must enter the collection of the National Gallery of Canada there was really very little knowledge of his work. I had missed the great monographic exhibitions at Karlsruhe in 1959. From the exhibition of chiaroscuro woodcuts at Paris and Rotterdam in 1965 and 1968, I knew him to be an imaginative and skilful artist. I had even retained an affection for the expressiveness of what I am told are his inflated and awkward late works such as the *Mercury* in Stockholm. When faced with the purchase of this newly discovered painting, I did make pilgrimages to see again the works that seemed to have the greatest affinity with *Eve, the Serpent and Death*: the very early *Knight, Death and a Maiden* in the Louvre (fig. 16); *Death and the Three Ages of Woman* in Vienna (fig. 17); and the two paintings of *Death and the Woman* in Basel (figs. 18 and 19). All four small works impressed me with Baldung's greatness and left me determined that Ottawa should acquire the small panel painting.

Ottawa has been drawn to small masterpieces. The small, low-ceilinged galleries of the theoretically temporary building occupied from 1960 provide them with a sympathetic background. But even when the Gallery was in the Victoria Memorial Museum Building with its vast, high-ceilinged spaces, its directors and curators were buying small works. This is true of the paintings bought through Agnew from Prince Liechtenstein, the serene Memling, the poignant Quentin Matsys, and the precious Chardins. It was tempting to find other small paintings to measure up to these, and in my time we did buy a small early *Tribute Money* by Rembrandt, a tiny Salvador Dali and the Baldung. The Baldung emphatically as much as these others has presence in spite of its scale.

The Baldung is also, like the other small masterpieces in Ottawa, exquisitely painted and in impeccable condition. This is, of course, part of its seduction. Undoubtedly Baldung was primarily, like most of his German contemporaries, a printmaker and draughtsman before he was a painter. He even began his panel painting as a drawing, hatching and cross-hatching as carefully as he would have done for a woodcut. That hatching is visible through the thin layers of the glaze of Eve's flesh. This form of construction makes the modelling as consistent as a work of sculpture in relief. At the same time, the line is predictably expressive. The contours describing Death may be incredibly disciplined, like the golden hatching on his back, but they are essentially tense and tortured. The rough lines of the bark of the tree indicate its texture. The smooth, uninterrupted curves of the snake have the power of a whip. On the other hand, the contours of Eve's body are exquisite. Admittedly they can be harshly descriptive around her neck, in the folds of the skin at her ankles or in the definition of her worn toes, but essentially they reveal an effort on this German artist's part toward a classical serenity of design. That classical serenity disappears, however, in the tumbled hair which falls back so that it leaves the oval face, the firm neck, and the shoulders tidily free; the hair has its own life – intense, wilful, convoluted – more in harmony with the figure of Death than with Eve's own smooth body.

Eve, the Serpent and Death is not just a linear work. The cream of Eve's flesh is luminous against the dark ground of the Garden of Eden, and the grey of the serpent is coldly ominous. In the figure of Death there are browns and golds that are repeated in Eve's hair. There is also some red in his flayed flesh that becomes stronger in the apple he holds and is repeated diagonally downward in Eve's lips, her nipples and the apple she conceals behind her back. The serpent's eye is also diabolically red.

Although the panel is smooth, and admirable because it is so smooth, there are the most graphic descriptions of textures. There is the finely scaled surface of the serpent against the rough bark of the tree. There is the electric life of Eve's hair against the smoothness of her skin. And there is the horror of bone and flayed skin and flesh of the figure of Death against Eve's pristinely smooth body. All of this is immaculately painted.

The seductions of such technical mastery are combined with such perfection of condition that the panel in itself has even greater sensual appeal. Mario Modestini, who cleaned the picture for Agnew, wrote of its condition: 'Rarely have I cleaned a sixteenth-century picture still so precise in definition, completely unrubbed, and with the quality of paint so preserved.' In Ottawa, X-raying by the Conservation Laboratory revealed tiny losses on the cheek and jaw of Death and on the trunk of the tree. Mervyn Ruggles, the Chief Conservator, could share Modestini's pleasure in the Baldung's condition. He was particularly enraptured by the glimpses of drawing on the gesso ground through the glazes of Eve's flesh.

The painting has another seduction, which is intellectual. Its subject is complex with more layers of meaning than even the title implies. According to Professor Koch, Baldung painted it between 1510 and 1512 – that is at the time of the High Renaissance in Rome and, more pertinently, at the peak of the Humanist revival in the North and a few years before Martin Luther ushered in the Reformation by posting his theses at Wittenberg in 1517. Very little is known about Baldung, but he was born a Catholic in Swabia about 1485 and died in Strasbourg a Protestant in 1545. From great ecclesiastic commissions such as the altarpiece for Freiburg Cathedral in 1512, he moved on to make woodcut portraits of Martin Luther in 1520 and 1521. Any connection with the great humanists such as Erasmus is

Figure 16 Hans Baldung Grün, *Knight, Death and a Maiden*, Musée du Louvre, Paris

undocumented, but he appears to have studied with Dürer between 1503 and 1507; and that artist, who admired Baldung sufficiently to take prints of his with him on a trip to the Netherlands in 1521, must have introduced this student to humanist ideas. On the other end of the spectrum, there is evidence that Baldung was interested in necromancy. His late (1544) woodcut, *The Bewitched Stablegroom*, has even been interpreted as an autobiographical study. Therefore late mediaeval witchcraft, the religious revolution and humanist ideas can all be brought together to explain this small painting.

Presumably the scene is laid in the Garden of Eden. And yet Eden is not a paradise but an impenetrable and dark, forbidding wood – frightening and mysterious, something to escape rather than to regret. Although less stuffed with symbols than the Eden in Dürer's famous engraving of 1504, *The Fall of Man*, upon which Dürer would have been working when Baldung

Figure 17 Hans Baldung Grün, *Death and the Three Ages of Woman*, Kunsthistorisches Museum, Vienna

Catholicism and emerging dissident Protestantism in the early sixteenth century are often conveyed in the image of Adam and Eve at the moment of temptation, as in Dürer's *Fall of Man* or Baldung's own chiaroscuro woodcut of the same subject from 1511. Occasionally Eve is shown alone with the symbols of the Garden, the tree, the serpent, and the apple as Baldung had shown her in a drawing of 1510 which is now in the Kunsthalle, Hamburg. There was often a theological ambiguity expressed in these representations of the concept of the fall of man and original sin. This is true of Dürer's engraving, in which the potential for the classically formed Eve and the Apollo-like Adam would seem to be greater after the Fall. Both Baldung's drawing of 1510 and his woodcut of 1511 show greater hesitancy on the part of his figures than do Dürer's; it is as if they were hapless victims making very uncertain steps into the unknown. They do not anticipate the spirit of *Eve, the Serpent and Death* except in the possible equation of female pulchritude with the potential for sin.

The unusual aspect of this representation of the Fall of Man is that Adam is replaced by an unmistakable figure of Death. Even if he holds up an apple, instead of an hourglass, the significance of the flayed body and skull-like head is clear. Baldung in all his work was fascinated by the concept of beautifully formed female flesh threatened by the corruption of Death. He had shown Death holding an hourglass over a figure of Vanitas, a comely young woman with luxuriant hair looking into a mirror, in *Death and the Three Ages of Woman* from about 1510 in Vienna. In two drawings he dated 1515, which are in Berlin, Death shows off a nude, in one case heroically beautiful and once again gazing into her mirror. Baldung's sense of the strongly erotic compulsion between female pulchritude and Death grew until in 1515 he painted the tiny *Death and the Woman* in Basel in which Death holds the woman tenderly and bites her chin, while she struggles in despair. In the Vienna painting and the Berlin drawing, the young woman seems unaware of the figure of Death. In the Basel painting she struggles. In Ottawa's – the only work in which she is identified as Eve by the serpent and the apple – she flirts with Death.

Indeed the Ottawa painting can be seen as growing out of the late medieval tradition of the Dance of Death. The positions of Eve and Death (if it were not for the intrusive serpent) could be those required for some formal dance, like the *pavane*. Death suspends an apple above her head either accusingly or triumphantly, and she holds her apple in a gesture, not unlike Dürer's Eve but more coyly, behind her back. The flirtatious provocation in that gesture, in her nipples, and in her raised eyebrows, complacent smile, and eyes turned knowingly and confidently toward the figure of Death suggest a special affinity with Death,

was his student, Baldung's is as ominous. Baldung falls within the same tradition. Eden was the price paid for knowledge or enlightenment and therefore a dark and mysterious place.

Out of this strange Eden emerges the serpent. In the Dürer he is clearly a snake, but he has insinuated himself around the branch of the tree so that he seems a perfectly organic and protected part of Eden. On the other hand, Baldung's serpent is a disturbingly dissident presence in colour, texture, and form. Whereas in the Dürer Eve offers the snake an apple with her right hand, here she touches his body with her left, while the serpent coils around the tree and, with his whippet-like head, gnaws the arm of the figure of Death.

The problems that the concept of original sin presented for

Figure 18 Hans Baldung Grün, *Death and the Woman*, Kunstmuseum, Basle

or perhaps we should say with Mortality. Professor Koch sees Death's gesture with the apple and his other hand grasping her wrist as admonitory and speculates that 'The personification of Death may also be seen as a representation of Adam himself as a corpse, the fate to which his body was destined at the Fall.' In any event the colour and the wildness of Eve's witchlike hair seem to bind her to Death. It is the serpent that is the alien presence as he gnaws at the wrist of Death as if he were protecting Eve.

We are left with certain theological problems. Certainly the painting is a *memento mori* – a reminder of the inevitability of death, even for flirtatious young women. Certainly it refers to the Fall – the sacrifice of eternal life and innocence for know-ledge. On the other hand, Eve seems beautiful but hardly innocent, and the world she inhabits more of an Endor than an Eden. It is as if by her own nature Eve had determined her own fall; the serpent is irrelevant. We have a painting, therefore, that questions the very dogma of original sin, an indication of the scepticism of the expanding Reformation.

Ottawa was fortunate enough to be able to acquire a beautiful painting in exquisite condition and one from an important period in the history of art that is poorly represented in America, but in which the National Gallery of Canada already had some strength. At the same time, it also acquired a provocative document in the history of ideas from the intellectual and religious ferment leading up to the Reformation.

Figure 19 Hans Baldung Grün, *Death and the Maiden*, Öffentliche Kunstsammlung, Basle

Adam Elsheimer, *Il Contento*, 11¾×16½ inches, negotiated with the
Treasury in lieu of Estate Duty, the National Gallery of Scotland,
Edinburgh, 1970

Gerard David, *The Crucifixion*, 26½×16¾ inches,
with E. V. Thaw & Co., to Walter P. Chrysler, Jr., 1976

Jan 'Velvet' Brueghel, *Landscape with Abraham and Isaac*,
18¾×26¾ inches, Private Collection, USA, 1976

Figure 20 Sir Peter Paul Rubens, *Deborah Kip, Wife of Sir Balthasar Gerbier, and Her Children*, 64½×69½ inches, National Gallery of Art, Washington, Andrew W. Mellon Fund, 1971

Rubens's
Madame Gerbier and Her Children

MICHAEL JAFFÉ

In 1973 the National Gallery of Art in Washington devoted its annual 'Studies in the History of Art' to a painting by Rubens which had been bought two years earlier from Agnew's with the Andrew W. Mellon Fund: *Deborah Kip, wife of Balthasar Gerbier, and her children*[1] (fig. 20). It was indeed a fortunate acquisition for the United States.

This masterpiece of portraiture celebrates tenderly those months from May 1629 to February 1630 during which Rubens was lodged by Royal command at York House in the Strand. There, to the Duchess of Buckingham's disgust, Balthasar Gerbier, Master of the Horse to her late husband, was still in lawful occupation. Rubens had come to Charles I with what was virtually his own 'project for the cessation of armes' between Great Britain and Spain, having been newly appointed by Philip IV as Secretary of the Council of the Netherlands in order that he might negotiate in London with some standing on behalf of both Philip and Philip's aunt the Infanta, Governess of the Spanish Netherlands. In pursuit of the same pacification, he had been in touch with Gerbier intermittently since their meeting in Paris in 1625, but hitherto in a clandestine fashion and abortively.

The portrait which he composed of Deborah Gerbier aged about thirty, her four eldest children clustered about her on the vine-clad terrace of a mansion, imagined above the Thames by the light of late afternoon, has not only a prime historical interest for Great Britain, but it is also an outstanding rarity within his whole production: a life-size family group, not of his own family. In this sense there is little to compare with it except his display of the Gonzaga rather larger than life in their altar-piece of 1604–5 for the Jesuit church in Mantua,[2] and his painting of 1613–4, now in London, of his friend *Jan Breughel and his family*.[3] Of the *Gerbier Family* now in Washington there are

copies, but no other seventeenth-century version save the one bought in Flanders in 1749 for Frederick, Prince of Wales; and that is no better than a workshop adaptation aggrandized by a considerable, but stylistically alien enlargement at the right[4] (fig. 21). When the original was shipped from London in 1971, the occasion was the first for at least 250 years that it had been outside England.

The earliest reference to the Washington painting appears to be in a letter from Rubens's second wife, Hélène Fourment, some years after his death. The widow wrote, probably in 1646, from Antwerp to a fellow citizen, the dealer Matthijs Musson, offering '*de Contrefeytsels van de Engelse mevrou met haer kinderen*'; a portrait valued at 600 guilders, and a description which fits no other known portrait by the master. Her offer implies either that the *Gerbier Family* always belonged to her husband, or, more likely, that it returned to him or to his family after his death. The sky is Titianesque; and the close configuration reflects, albeit with full-length figures, that of Titian's *Allegory of Avalos*, which Rubens saw at Whitehall as *The Marquess de Gwasto* in the royal collection (fig. 22). At York House, besides drawing such studies of the Gerbier children as he required for the large *Picture of an Emblin wherein the differences and ensuances between peace and warres is Shewed*, his handsome present to Charles I[5] (fig. 23), Rubens is likely to have adumbrated some-how – probably by an oil sketch – the composition for portrayal of his host's family. He may even have started work on the actual canvas, the nodal piece around which another five strips were to be joined. Nevertheless, since the Gerbier family resided officially in Brussels from June 1631 to 1640, since the elder children appear in the portrait group slightly older than in the allegory, and since Barbara Gerbier wears Netherlandish, rather than English, dress of about 1630, her cap in the French

Figure 21 Sir Peter Paul Rubens, Detail of *Peace and War* showing the Gerbier Children, National Gallery, London

fashion, Rubens's completion of the work in its definitive form is unlikely to have taken place until after the first year or so of his own return to Antwerp in March 1630.[6] Moreover, since it is not listed in the mortuary inventory taken of Rubens's works of art, it may well have been Gerbier property from about 1631 until mid or late 1640, and then sold by Gerbier to Hélène Rubens on his final departure from Flanders. That Gerbier himself does not appear on it is unexplained. Lack of personal vanity is an unlikely reason. Would his absence give the portrait better prospects of sale? Was a pendant contemplated, with him in some other quality than that of husband and father?

The history of the painting becomes entirely clear from 1724. On 24 April that year George Vertue saw it being sold by Cock at Lord Radnor's house in St James's Square as 'A. van Dyck, *A Large Family Picture*', Lord Burlington bidding £500 for it but being outbid by Mr Scawen at 505 guineas. Vertue's attribution hesitated between Rubens and Van Dyck. We can only surmise whether it had belonged to the 2nd Earl of Radnor's father, who had been Lord Privy Seal to Charles II and a rich collector. Vertue records that in the possession of Mr Scawen it was copied by Ranelagh Barret for 'a relation of Mr Scawen'. This copy is untraced. The original was bought in at £310 in the Scawen sale of January 1743, being bought afterwards by a Mr Burroughs, by 'A Gent. of the Law' and eventually by Samson Gideon. It was copied in watercolour in 1749, with some arbitrary extension of the composition, this copy being signed and dated by William Jett; and by then it may have been in Gideon's possession. It was certainly so by 1735, the date of a mezzotint engraving by James McArdell, who used Jett's copy and its extensions, and recorded the presence of the original at Belvedere, Gideon's house in Kent. It passed to Gideon's son, who became Baron Eardley. It was called to my attention in October 1962, in the house of one of the great financier's descendants, Colonel David Fremantle, and mentioned by me three years later in a review in *The Burlington Magazine*.[7] The picture, long known to Agnew's, was acquired from the Fremantle family. It is noteworthy that on 30 June 1860 it had been sent from Belvedere by Culling Eardley, the religious philanthropist, to Christie's, dubbed *The Mistress of the Duke of Buckingham and Her Children. The Times* of 2 July reported that 'it was put up at 1,000 guineas and advanced 500 guineas at each bidding, till it reached the enormous amount of 7,500 guineas, at which sum it was knocked down to Mr Ward. Great applause followed the adjudication'. This was the highest recorded price for a Rubens in the sale-room: but Ward was a buying-in name.

Vertue remembered the Radnor sale of 1724, particularly when in 1749 he was asked to advise the Prince of Wales on the purchase of the version now at Windsor. A sketch of that picture on offer was sent from Southern Flanders, the subject identified as *Sir Balthasar Arundel and his family*. The Prince also consulted both Joseph Goupy, who had taught him to paint in watercolours, and General Guise who had served under Marlborough, and who was to leave an important collection of drawings and paintings to Christ Church, Oxford. Vertue, who inclined to think Van Dyck the author of this bizarrely titled portrait group, was pleased to identify the likeness of Gerbier from engravings, and to confirm the identification by the three *gerbes* with which the shield impressed on the flowerpot was charged, as appropriate to Gerbier's patent of knighthood. He was less pleased when Goupy and Guise returned from their reconnaissance abroad with the picture rechristened *Sir Balthazar Buckingham or Sheffield.* Apparently unknown to any of these connoisseurs was a description in an inventory drawn in Paris after the death in 1662 of Cardinal Mazarin: '*Un autre faict par Rubens, sur toile, représentant une Famille de neuf enfants dont les père et mère sont debout, haulte de six piedz six poulces et large de neuf piedz trois poulces.*' Except that Deborah Gerbier, as she is depicted, is seated, the description fits.

The Windsor (?Mazarin) version, in the Royal Collection since 1776, was evidently commissioned by Gerbier in Flanders for his own satisfaction, rather than for resale. In the first stage of execution, to judge by style and circumstance of the mid 1630s, a member of the Rubens studio was employed to copy Deborah, together with George, Susan, Mary and the baby named for his godfather Charles I, and to add Balthasar at the left, where his wife's back was straightened to accommodate him, and two little girls, perhaps twins, at the right. Between 22 October 1638, when Gerbier received his knighthood from Charles I, and 1640, when he left Flanders, he increased the size of his picture by employing yet another unidentified, but more individual painter, not one trained in the Rubens studio, to introduce three more of his children and, on a stone balustrade, an armorial flowerpot. This act of familial pride made it impossible to represent realistically the respective ages of the groups of children: George, for example, was by this time a captain in Lord Craven's troops championing the Winter Queen. These additions to the second version, however confusing, would have made the original painting by Rubens that much less satisfactory to the Gerbier as their family portrait; and, short of cash, they would have been the readier to realize its value by private treaty with the Rubens heirs.

Perhaps while the Washington original was in Rubens's studio being imitated for Gerbier, the author of quite another *Family Portrait* may have taken the opportunity, as Mr John Walker has suggested, to appropriate what he wanted of Rubens's invention. The boy in this group by the so-called

Figure 22 Sir Peter Paul Rubens, *The Gerbier Family*,
reproduced by gracious permission of Her Majesty the Queen

'Maître de Ribaucourt' draws the curtain with his right hand, as in the Washington picture (X-rays of which show it was the boy's left hand originally), whereas in the Windsor picture the 'uncorrected' left hand was used. Deborah Gerbier's beautiful green skirt sprigged with flowers is plainer and tamer in the Windsor adaptation; and in that the fat red tassel of the curtain, more or less inconspicuous against the vine trellis in the original, hangs obtrusively (as the X-ray shows that it once did in the original) silhouetted above Susan Gerbier's head. Such points then can have been of no great moment to Rubens who understandably may not have wished to involve himself, once the original was resolved, in any close supervision of an adaptation of it for Gerbier. A seventeenth-century copy of the figure of Susan Gerbier, which, according to Vertue, belonged to Jonathan Richardson, and which is now in Lord Spencer's collection at Althorp, shows her wearing a coil of hair as she

does in the Washington painting, and such as does not appear in the Windsor painting. This is yet another pointer to the primacy of the Washington picture.

The late Ludwig Burchard appears to have been in doubt of this. He wrote of the Windsor picture: 'The composition developed in three stages: the central group of the mother and four children was painted by Rubens in London in 1629–30, when he was staying with Gerbier; the children advancing up the steps and the figure of Gerbier are later additions in a style close to Rubens; the area including the three children on the right is a latter addition in an entirely different hand. A version of the original composition is in the Fremantle Collection, and of the little girl at her mother's knee at Althorp.' Gregory Martin reckoned in 1970, when cataloguing *Peace and War* for the National Gallery, that the Windsor picture 'may at least in part be by Rubens'. He may not have had first-hand knowledge of the Fremantle picture at the time of writing. Such opinions may have been influential in the decision not to withhold licence under any of the Waverley criteria to export that.

In the *Corpus Rubenianum Ludwig Burchard: Portraits I*, published in 1977 in Brussels, that is some years after the painting had undergone treatment by the late Richard Buck for the National Gallery of Art, Frances Huemer wrote that: 'In addition to the careless peripheral painting, the painting and drawing of the heads is unconvincing, often with a splotchy overpainting. Not only is the hair stringy and fussy (compare the impressionistic hair of the little girl in the *Peace and War*; in Madame Gerbier's hair the background is a flat gray with superimposed reddish locks – but the brushstrokes on the face are dry and hard. The irises of the eyes are painted so that they appear almost a solid brown with circular centres, with even lighter outer parts. This is contrary to the way Rubens paints the iris of the eye with more broken contours of light. Mainly in both the Windsor and Washington versions, the faces lack that beautiful vibrancy of the faces in the *Peace and War*. The Washington painting may be a workshop copy never completed. Its strengths are those taken from Rubens: the colour scheme and the composition. Its weaknesses are in the painting itself, a deadness of areas, and a certain deadness of expression. It has a fatal lack of unity in the construction of forms.'

Deadness and lack of unity are thus seen in the aftermath of a cleaning imprudent in approach to the problems actual or potential, as revealed by Mr Buck's own published report, and correspondingly insensitive to the optical effects. What Vasari wrote of Titian's advanced style is highly relevant to Rubens's painting of the early 1630s. After 350 years the boldly and freely painted surface of the Washington version was in all essentials well preserved; but something needs to be done to bring its parts into keeping again. A clumsy relining calls attention to the joins in the canvas; insufficient appreciation of the way in which Rubens matched his ground tone on the added strips to the nodal piece is another cause of the present lamentable discontinuity of impression; the dryness and hardness, remarked by Miss Huemer, are functions of unskilled varnishing. Much could be remedied.

Reviewing the 'Loan Exhibition of Flemish and Belgian Art' at the Royal Academy in 1927, when the harmony of the picture was marred not by cleaning but by dirty and discoloured varnish, Roger Fry wrote of *Madame Gerbier*: 'Rubens has conceived it in a manner all his own. . . . The group is admirably balanced. The poses continue to make an almost sculptural unity.' Rubens was not, for Fry, the most sympathetic of European Masters. But Fry could recognize a masterpiece when he saw one.

Figure 23 Titian, *Allegory of Avalos*, . Musée du Louvre, Paris

[1] 1973 Studies in the History of Art: contributions by Wolfgang Stechow, 'Peter Paul Rubens's *Deborah Kip, Wife of Sir Balthasar Gerbier, and Her Children*'; Clovis Whitfield, 'Balthasar Gerbier, Rubens, and George Vertue'; Richard D. Buck, 'Rubens: Examination and Treatment'; Robert L. Feller, 'Rubens: Technical Examination of the Pigments and Paint Layers'; Bernard Keisch and Robert L. Callagham, 'Rubens: Investigation by Lead Isotope Mass Spectrometry'. The publication by Mr Whitfield of the Vertue material is of notable importance to establishing the provenance of the Fremantle-Washington picture.

[2] Ugo Bazzotti, 'La Pala della Trinità', in *Rubens a Mantova*, Mantua, Palazzo Ducale, 1977.

[3] H. Vlieghe, 'Het portret van Jan Breughel en zÿn gezin door P. P. Rubens', in *Bulletin des Musées Royaux des Beaux-Arts de Belgique*, 1966–3, 177ff.

[4] Frances Huemer, 'Portraits I', in *Corpus Rubenianum Ludwig Burchard*, London 1977, no. 14, gives the full literature and references to that year.

[5] Gregory Martin, *National Gallery Catalogues. The Flemish School (c.1600–c.1900)*, London, 1970, no. 46, 116–125.

[6] John Walker, 'Two paintings of the Gerbier Family', in *Art Studies for an Editor: 25 Essays in Memory of Milton S. Fox*, New York, 1975, 245–54. Sir Oliver Millar's observations about the apparent age of the children and the nationality of Lady Gerbier's costume are included in this.

[7] Michael Jaffé, *Burlington Magazine*, 1965, 381, no. 146.

Sir Peter Paul Rubens, *Samson and Delilah*, 72¾×81 inches, purchased on
behalf of the Trustees of the National Gallery, the National Gallery,
London, 1980

Sir Peter Paul Rubens, *Samson and Delilah*, 21×23¼ inches,
Cincinnati Art Museum, The Harry S. and Eva Belle Leyman Fund, 1972

Sir Peter Paul Rubens, *Holy Women with Angels*, 34¹/₂×42¹/₄ inches, Norton
Simon Foundation, 1972

Sir Peter Paul Rubens, *Constantine and the Labarum*, 13¾×10⅞ inches, Private Collection, England, 1980

Sir Peter Paul Rubens, *The Triumph of Constantine*, 15×11½ inches, Private Collection, USA, 1980

Sir Anthony Van Dyck, *A Genoese Nobleman*, 29×24 inches,
William A. Coolidge Collection, Cambridge, Massachusetts, 1970

Sir Anthony Van Dyck, *Agostini Pallavicini*, 86¹/₄××56¹/₄ inches,
The J. Paul Getty Museum, Malibu, California, 1968

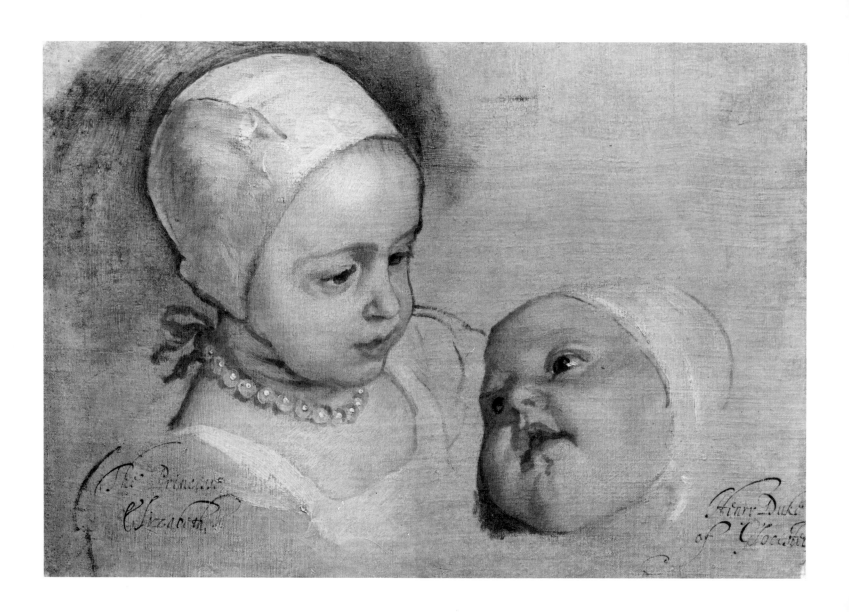

Sir Anthony Van Dyck, *Princess Elizabeth and Princess Anne, the Daughters of Charles I*,
11¾×16¾ inches, Private Collection, England, 1977

Jacob Jordaens, *Christ Taken in the Garden of Gethsemane*, 88¾×97 inches, with Rudoph J. Heinemann to The Cleveland Museum of Art, Purchase, Leonard C. Hanna, Jr., Bequest, 1970

Maerten van Heemskerck, *A Lady with Spindle and Distaff*,
40¾×32¾ inches, Collection Thyssen-Bornemisza, Lugano, 1970

Jan van Goyen, *The Landing Stage*, 14½×13½ inches,
Private Collection, USA, 1976

Jan van de Capelle, *Shipping in a Calm*, 16×21¼ inches,
Private Collection, England, 1969

Salomon van Ruysdael, *A River Landscape with a Ferry*, 20½×33 inches,
Private Collection, England, 1971

Jacob Ruisdael, *Castle Bentheim*, 24×29½ inches,
The Collection of James Fairfax, 1979

Jacob Ruisdael, *The Entrance to a Port in Stormy Weather*,
38½×51¾ inches, Private Collection, USA, 1977

Philips de Koninck, *An Extensive Landscape*, 54¼××66¼ inches,
negotiated with the Treasury in lieu of Estate Duty,
The National Gallery, London, 1971

Aelbert Cuyp, *A River Landscape with the Town of Merwede*, 28×36 inches,
Private Collection, England, 1978

Aelbert Cuyp, *Landscape with a View of the Valkhof, Nijmegen*, 44½×65 inches, bought from the estate of the late
L. R. Bradbury in 1972, with the aid of a contribution from the National Art-Collections Fund in recognition of
the services of the Earl of Crawford and Balcarres to the Fund and the National Galleries of Scotland, The
National Gallery of Scotland, Edinburgh

Rembrandt van Rijn, *Man in a Fur-lined Coat*, 44×33½ inches,
The Toledo Museum of Art, Clarence Brown Fund, 1977

Michael Sweerts, *Head of a Girl*, 17×14½ inches,
negotiated with the Treasury in lieu of Estate Duty.
Placed on loan to Leicestershire Museum and Art Gallery,
Leicester, in 1971, donated 1975

Pieter Claesz, *A Banquet Still-life*, 34×27½ inches,
Private Collection, UK, 1968

Jan Steen, *The Wedding Party*, 18×14⅛ inches,
The Collection of James Fairfax, 1974

Adriaen van Ostade, *A Peasant Family in an Interior*, 13½×12 inches,
Private Collection, USA, 1975

Jan van der Heyden, *An Architectural Fantasy*, 18½×27½ inches, National
Gallery of Art, Washington, Ailsa Mellon Bruce Fund, 1968

Figure 24 Bartolome–Esteban Murillo, *Don Justino de Neve*, 81⅛×51 inches, The National Gallery, London. Purchased through Agnew's, 1979

Murillo's
Don Justino de Neve

ALLAN BRAHAM

The National Gallery acquired in 1979 the most famous of Murillo's full-length portraits, his painting of Don Justino de Neve (fig. 24), formerly in the Lansdowne collection, which represents one of the few aspects of Murillo's art not already shown to advantage at Trafalgar Square.[1] One of the comparatively rare surviving portraits by the artist, it is the only seated full-length he is known to have painted, and a picture, moreover, that has gained appreciably from restoration (carried out before acquisition). The style of the portrait and its subtle colouring are now much more clearly apparent than hitherto, as are the alterations made by the artist in the course of creating it; the dated inscription panel (fig. 28) is fully visible for the first time in many years.

The picture was first mentioned in print by Palomino (1715), who gave it precedence over other portraits by the artist. He explained that the painting had been bequeathed to the Hospital of the Venerables in Seville in the Will of Don Justino, and, like other writers, he drew attention to the dog at the sitter's feet, an English lap-dog (*una perilla inglese* – a pug?), so life-like in appearance that it set real dogs snarling and barking (fig. 26).[2] According to Ponz (1780), the portrait was in the ante-refectory of the hospital, and Ceán Bermúdez stated that it had been painted to mark Murillo's gratitude to Don Justino who had been instrumental in commissioning his paintings in the church of S. Maria la Blanca and in the Venerables itself.[3]

The portrait is first recorded for certain in England in the 1818 exhibition at the British Institution, where it was lent by the collector George Watson Taylor, M.P.[4] According to William Buchanan it had been imported by Delahante about 1804 and sold to Taylor for 1000 guineas;[5] but the date, at least, must be wrong, since the portrait was one of the 999 paintings (forty-three attributed to Murillo) collected together in the Seville Alcázar in 1810 and destined for the Museum of Spanish painting being planned by Joseph Bonaparte, King of Spain.[6] Another picture in this collection, also from the Venerables, was Murillo's *Immaculate Conception,* now in the Prado, which later passed to Maréchal Soult. A few years previously, the Paris dealer Le Brun had visited Seville and is reliably stated to have made an unsuccessful offer of 20,000 francs for the portrait.[7] Presumably it came to London in the early 1810s, possibly through Delahante, although it is not traceable in any of the principal Delahante sales of the period. After being exhibited in 1818, it next appeared in the Watson Taylor sale of 1823.[8] The portrait was withdrawn at the comparatively high figure of 910 guineas, and put up for sale again in the auction of Watson Taylor's possessions at Erlestoke Park in 1832, where it was bought by Lord Lansdowne for 480 guineas.[9]

Amongst the many printed comments on the painting, reflecting the overwhelming popularity of Murillo during the course of the nineteenth century, two in particular reveal the qualities for which Murillo was then esteemed. His gift for creating atmospheric effects is brought out in the 1823 sale catalogue: 'An opening from the apartment to a Garden or Terrace behind him, admits a freshness and air that contribute a very sweet relief to the simple colouring of the Picture.' Waagen, who had seen the portrait at Bowood, also praised its tonality and noted how far the appearance of the sitter contributed to the success of the portrait: 'Portrait of an ecclesiastic; of delicate features, and of earnest and dignified character and beautiful hands, seated in an easy position; at his feet a dog. In point of elevation of conception, delicacy of drawing, admirable keeping in silvery tones, and careful execution, extending equally to the accessories, among which is a clock, this is one of the finest pictures I know by the master.'[10]

Figure 25
Detail of figure 24

Figure 26
Detail of figure 24

Figure 27
Detail of figure 24

Figure 28
Detail of figure 24

'Silvery tones' have now indeed emerged from beneath a golden varnish after the cleaning of the portrait, and the range of its colour is not the least remarkable of the picture's qualities. Against the shifting green and grey of the background of landscape and architecture, the warmer tone of the wooden chair and four shades of pink and red are juxtaposed: brightest of all is the scarlet of the bow around the neck of the dog: the fabric of the chair is a sombre red, the floor a grey pink and the curtain a striking purple-red, where a purer crimson might be expected in a more conventional portrait. Level with the landscape on the left is the green table cloth with its still-life of clock and bell and book. Here the influence of Titian on the art of Murillo seems particularly apparent, although in Titian's portrait of the Duchess of Urbino the sitter's pet dog was allowed to lie upon the table beside the clock (a model of patient fidelity), and the clock itself in Murillo's portrait, registering the time as ten to four, has a markedly ecclesiastical air (fig. 27). The silver bell is an item that not even Titian had thought of introducing into any known portrait, though a bell sometimes appears in Roman ecclesiastical portraits, notably in Raphael's *Leo X and his Nephews*.

Don Justino undoubtedly had real claims to the marks of learning, authority and affectionate respect that Murillo so discreetly introduced into the portrait. A canon and prebendary of the Cathedral of Seville, he was not only a patron of the artist – commissioning the S. Maria la Blanca paintings of 1662–5 and those of the Venerables of 1678 – but also one who became a close friend.[11] As has long been known, Don Justino acted as an executor of Murillo's Will in 1682, together with his son Gaspar and pupil Pedro della Villavicencio.[12] The portrait has generally been thought to date from the period when Murillo was painting his other works for the Venerables, but the inscription on the portrait, now uncovered by cleaning, indicates the year 1665; and this much earlier date accords better with the style of the picture. The head in particular (fig. 25) is distinctly less 'vaporous' than later heads by Murillo; for example, that of the National Gallery's *Self-portrait*. But it has the same degree of intensity, deriving from the calculated, almost proto-Goyaesque, spontaneity, of the handling.

The coat-of-arms and the inscription (fig. 28) appear to be early additions to the painting, indistinct in modelling and competing with the head of the sitter in the composition of the portrait. The arms are those of the Neve (left) and Chaves (right) families, and though Don Justino's surname is usually given as Neve y Yevenes, it appears as Neve y Chaves in Murillo's inventory. The inscription itself, in poorer Latin than the equally full inscription of the late *Self-portrait*, gives Murillo as the artist and the sitter's age as forty: 'ETATIS SVÆ. 40/Bar-

Figure 29 Barolome-Esteban Murillo, *Don Andres de Andrade y Col*, The Metropolitan Museum of Art, New York

tholome Murillo Romulensis/Præcirca obsequium desiderio pingebat/A.M.[D.] C.L.X.V.' 'Romulensis' must refer to the Roman name for Seville, *Colonia Romulensis*, while 'obsequium' presumably alludes not literally to obsequies, but to the sitter's employment of Murillo, so that the third line would mean, roughly: Murillo/was painting (this) at the request (of the sitter) while in (his) service.[13]

Such a reading is intelligible in relation to the dating, 1665, since in that year Murillo completed his canvases for S. Maria la Blanca.[14] This commission no doubt had a distinctly personal relevance to Don Justino, whose surname, Neve, echoes the dedication of the church to St Mary of the Snows (S. Maria ad Nieves) referring to the miraculous foundation of S. Maria Maggiore, the mother church in Rome.

The painting is thus, together with the portrait of Don Andrés de Andrade (fig. 29), one of the artist's earliest known portraits and, though Murillo had already painted for the Cathedral of Seville full-length seated figures of saints composed with almost Van Dyckian assurance, part of the strength of the portrait of Don Justino undoubtedly lies in the slightly naïve directness of the image, which lacks some of the assurance that Murillo later gained as a portraitist, though the degree of swagger needed for a full-length standing portrait was never fully in his power to convey. The sitter, who was probably small in stature, is not shown from a low view point, or amplified in size by the expansive draperies customarily introduced in seventeenth-century ecclesiastical portraits. It is only through the treatment of the head that the subject was made effectively in command of his surroundings. Originally the setting was more timidly composed, and the two major changes visible in the picture are the lowering of the curtain, and the enlargement of the green table cloth, which originally fell to a line at the level of the sitter's knees.[15] The care evident in the presentation is not unrelated to the pious character of the image, which in turn imparts to the portrait Murillo's strength as a devotional artist.

Reproduced from The Burlington Magazine,
March 1980, by kind permission of the Editor

[1] Canvas, 206 × 129.5 cm. Acquired from the Trustees of the Bowood Collection through Agnew's. C.B. Curtis: *Velasquez and Murillo*, 1883, pp. 297–8 (no. 470); William Stirling: *Annals of the Artists of Spain*, 1848, II, pp. 884–5. Exhibited with other paintings from the Lansdowne collection at Agnew's, 1954–5, pp. 22–3 (no. 35); no. 13 in the 1897 catalogue of the collection, by George E. Ambrose (p. 66).

[2] Antonio Palomino: *El Museo Pictórico* (1715–23), III, p. 432 (1797 ed., III, 625).

[3] Antonio Ponz: *Viage de España,* IX (1780), 123, Juan Augustín Ceán Bermúdez: *Diccionario histórico . . . de las Bellas Artes en España*, IV, 1800, p. 60, *and Carta . . . sobre el estilo y gusto de la escuela sevillana*, 1806, pp. 93–4.

[4] No. 36 ('Portrait of Fosco Neivis – Murillo: G. W. Taylor, Esq., M.P.').

[5] William Buchanan: *Memoirs of Painting*, 1824, II, pp. 190 and 193 (no. 14). According to Edward Davies: *The Life of Bartolomé E. Murillo*, 1819, p. 92, note, the portrait was 'brought to England by a French gentleman, and sold by Mr H. Phillips to Mr Watson Taylor'.

[6] See M. Gómez Imaz: *Inventario de los cuadros sustraídos por el Gobierno Intruso en Sevilla (año 1810)*, 1917 (2nd ed.), p. 148 (no. 193): '*otro de igual tamano (2½ varas × 1¾), un retrato del Canonigo Nebes*'.

[7] F. Quillet: *Dictionnaire des peintres espagnols*, 1816, p. 100; as he explains, Quillet served as interpreter for Le Brun, whose visits to Spain were apparently in 1807 and 1808 (Buchanan, *op. cit.*, II, p. 250).

[8] Christie's, 13–14 June 1823, lot 51 (p. 12 second day).

[9] Auctioned by George Robins, 9 July 1823 and following days, No. 77 on 24 July (p. 160).

[10] G. F. Waagen: *Treasures of Art in Great Britain*, 1854, III, p. 160. The absence of the painting in Seville is lamented by Felix Gonzalez de Leon: *Noticia artistica . . . de esta . . . Ciudad de Sevilla*, 1844, II, pp. 162–3.

[11] The friendship of Murillo and Don Justino is noted in most early sources (see above).

[12] For the inventory see D. Angulo Iniguez in *Boletin de la Real Academia de la Historia*, 1966, pp. 147–80. A search in the *Actas capitulares* of the Biblioteca Capitular y Colombina in Seville, undertaken by Don Pedro Rubio and kindly communicated by the Director, has established that Don Justino de Neve is recorded as '*Coadjutor de una canongia*' on 17 March 1646 and as a Canon in 1658; his death in 1685 is recorded but not the year of his birth.

[13] I am particularly grateful to my colleagues Mrs Cooke (Margaret Jones) and Paul Spencer-Longhurst for helping me to translate the inscription, and to Michael Levey for the elucidation of 'Romulensis'.

[14] D. Angulo Iniguez in *Archivo de Arte Espanol*, 1975, pp. 157–8. The portrait is given an early dating ('1655–65') by A. Mayer: *Murillo (Klassiker der Kunst)*, 1923, pl. 229.

[15] X-ray photographs of the head, the hands and the dog show no evidence of any alterations in these areas of the picture.

Francisco Zurbaran, *Birth of the Virgin*, 55¼×43 inches,
with E. V. Thaw & Co., to the Norton Simon Foundation, 1970

Francisco José de Goya y Lucientes, *St Ambrose*, 77³⁄₄×44¹⁄₂ inches,
with Rudoph J. Heinemann to the Cleveland Museum of Art.
Purchase, Leonard C. Hanna, Jr., Bequest, 1969

Francisco José de Goya y Lucientes, *El Sueno*, 17½×30 inches,
National Gallery of Ireland, 1970

Nicolas Poussin, *The Holy Family with St John*, 66½×48 inches,
The Toledo Museum of Art, Gift of Edward Drummond Libbey, 1976

Nicolas Poussin, *The Martyrdom of Saint Erasmus*, 39³/₈×29¹/₈ inches,
with E. V. Thaw and Co., to the National Gallery of Canada, Ottawa,
1972

Claude Gellée, called Le Lorrain, *Landscape with Piping Herdsmen*,
11×13½ inches, The Collection of James Fairfax, 1973

Claude Gellée, called Le Lorrain, *View of La Crescenza*, 15×22½ inches,
with E. V. Thaw and Co. to the Metropolitan Museum of Art, New York.
Purchased by the Annenberg Fund Inc., Gift, 1978

Claude Gellée, called Le Lorrain, *Rebecca Taking Leave of Her Father*,
23¼×31 inches, Nationalmuseum, Stockholm, 1974

Nicolas de Largillière, *Nicolas Coustou*, 53¼×41 inches,
Staatliche Museen Preussischer Kulturbesitz Gemäldegalerie Berlin (West),
1979

Jean Baptiste François Pater, *Les Plaisirs du Camp*, 11½×15½ inches,
Staatliche Kunsthalle, Karlsruhe, 1967

Claude Monet, *Terrace at Sainte-Adresse*, 38½×51 inches,
The Metropolitan Museum of Art, New York. Purchased with special contributions
and purchase funds given or bequeathed by Friends of the Museum, 1967

Claude Monet, *Vetheuil*, 19⅜×23⅞ inches, Southampton Art Gallery, 1975

Paul Cézanne, *Head of the Artist's Son, Paul*, 8³/₄×6¹/₂ inches,
Mr William Bowmore, Newcastle, Australia, 1978

Georges Seurat, *La Luzerne, Saint-Denis*, 25½×31¾ inches,
The National Gallery of Scotland, Edinburgh, 1973

Richard Wilson, R.A., *The Thames from Richmond with a View of Syon House*, 40³⁄₈×54 inches, Neue Pinakothek, Munich, 1978

Richard Wilson, R.A., *Dinas Bran, near Llangollen*, 71³/₄×96¹/₂ inches,
Yale Center for British Art, Paul Mellon Collection, 1972

George Stubbs, A.R.A., *A Cheetah and Stag with Two Indians*,
71×107 inches, Manchester City Art Galleries, 1970

George Stubbs, A.R.A., *A Man with a Grey Hack and Greyhound*,
18×27 inches, Private Collection, USA, 1977

Samuel Scott, *The Building of Westminster Bridge*, 27×46 inches,
Yale Center for British Art, Paul Mellon Collection, 1974

Sir Joshua Reynolds, P.R.A., *Mrs Abington as 'Miss Prue' in 'Love for Love'*,
Yale Center for British Art, Paul Mellon Collection, 1972

Sir Joshua Reynolds, *Lawrence Sterne*, 49×39½ inches, The Trustees of the National Portrait Gallery. Purchased with help from an anonymous benefactor, the National Art-Collections Fund, the Pilgrim Trust, Her Majesty's Government and the results of a public appeal, 1975

Thomas Gainsborough, R.A., *Joshua Grigby*, 50×40 inches,
Staatliche Museen Preussischer Kulturbesitz Gemäldegalerie Berlin (West),
1980

Thomas Gainsborough, R.A., *John and Henry Truman Villebois*,
61×51 inches, Private Collection, England, 1979

Thomas Gainsborough, R.A., *A Mountain Landscape with Shepherd and Sheep*, 46½×58¼ inches, Bayerisches Landesbank, Munich, on loan to the Neue Pinakothek, Munich, 1978

Thomas Gainsborough, R.A., *A Peasant Girl Gathering Faggots*,
66½×48½ inches, Manchester City Art Galleries, 1978

Johann Zoffany, R.A., *George, 3rd Earl Cowper and the Gore Family*,
29½×37 inches, Yale Center for British Art,
Paul Mellon Collection, 1977

John Singleton Copley, R.A., *Portrait of Richard Heber*,
64⅞×51 inches, Yale Center for British Art,
Paul Mellon Collection, 1979

Sir Thomas Lawrence, P.R.A., *Richard Payne Knight*, 50×40 inches, negotiated with the Treasury in lieu of Estate Duty. Placed on loan to the Whitworth Art Gallery, University of Manchester, in 1970, donated 1975

John Hoppner, R.A., *Paulet St John Mildmay*,
50×40 inches, Private Collection, England, 1980

Ben Marshall, *Colonel Henry Campbell Shooting on a Moor*,
33⅞×40 inches, Private Collection, USA, 1980

John Crome, *The Beaters*, 21½×33½ inches,
The National Gallery of Scotland, Edinburgh, 1970

John Sell Cotman, *Windmills and Marshes*, 21⅞×36¼ inches,
Yale Center for British Art, Paul Mellon Collection, 1973

Figure 30 John Constable, *Salisbury Cathedral from the Bishop's Grounds*
(1811), 29×36 inches, National Gallery of Canada, Ottawa, 1976

Constable's
Salisbury Cathedral

GRAHAM REYNOLDS

'. . . so much does this city, by a singular chance, associate to my life.'
Constable writing about Salisbury to John Fisher in November 1825

John Constable's introduction to the cathedral city of Salisbury took place in 1811. It was to be the first link in a chain of events which led to his painting the oil sketch *Salisbury Cathedral from the Bishop's Grounds* (fig. 30), which is now in the collection of the National Gallery of Canada.

When he first saw Salisbury, Constable was thirty-five years old and at a turning point in his career. He had not had an easy time establishing himself as an artist. Born in East Bergholt, Suffolk, the fourth child and second son of a prosperous corn merchant, Constable had somewhat disappointed his family with his choice of profession. His dedication to landscape painting did little to help, since it was not fashionable in the England of that time.

When he visited Salisbury in 1811, however, things had begun to change. He had recently achieved the breakthrough into a more natural method of painting for which he had been searching. Such oil sketches as the *Epsom* of June 1809 in the Tate Gallery, London, and the *View towards the Rectory, East Bergholt, at Sunrise* of September 1810, show that he had now mastered the art of rendering nuances of light and colour, and had shaken off mannerisms derived from the imitation of other painters. On a larger scale, his oils of *Malvern Hall, Warwickshire* of 1809, and the *Dedham Vale: Morning* of 1811, in the collection of Major Sir Richard Proby, foreshadow in their serene accomplishment the assurance of his most mature works.

The invitation to visit Salisbury therefore came to a man who had reason to believe that his painting was going well, even though the public was little disposed to recognize his merit. He had already abandoned the practice of deliberately travelling outside his own homeland in search of picturesque scenery. He only added fresh subject-matter to his range of landscape if it was made vital to him by personal associations and the presence of his friends. His journey to Salisbury fulfilled these conditions.

His host was a friend of long standing, then the Bishop of Salisbury, Dr John Fisher. When they had first met in 1798 Fisher was fifty years old and was visiting one of the parishes he held in those pluralistic times,[1] at Langham in Essex, near Constable's birthplace. At that meeting Constable was twenty-two and, although absorbed in drawing and sketching, had not yet decided to make art his profession.

Himself an amateur of painting, Fisher encouraged Constable in a number of ways. He maintained a residence in London, and it was there that he kept in touch with the artist during the first decade of the nineteenth century. The Bishop's wife was equally attracted; she described Constable as looking like one of the younger figures in Raphael, with a guileless countenance.

Constable had established a fairly regular routine whereby he spent the winter months in London, painting his pictures for the next Royal Academy exhibition. After that opened in May he returned as quickly as possible to Suffolk, where he could continue his study of the familiar countryside. In 1811 he varied this programme by accepting the Bishop's invitation to stay at the Palace in Salisbury, going there in mid-September and staying for three weeks. He was well looked after and wrote to the girl whom he hoped to marry, Maria Bicknell: 'The great kindness (I may almost say affection) that the good Bishop and Mrs Fisher have so long shown me was never more exerted in an unusual degree to make everything agreeable to me.'

At this period, the glories of the architecture of Salisbury were well recognized. It had been built in a remarkably short space of time, in the thirty-eight years between 1220 and 1258, and this rapid construction resulted in an unusual uniformity of

Figure 31 *Salisbury Cathedral from the South-West.* (11 and 12 September 1811).
Black and white chalk on grey paper, Victoria & Albert Museum, London

design. (The 404-foot spire which is its crowning excellence was added 100 years after the foundation.) The interior had been scoured into bleakness in the late eighteenth century by the restorations of Wyatt, but the chief interest to tourist and landscape painter alike was the exterior, impressive near at hand and dramatic at a distance. Constable, coming as he did from the flat lands of East Anglia, where large church towers are often the only vertical accent apart from the sky, was accustomed to such impressions; even so he was enraptured by the situation of the majestic building, the mellowed warmth of its stone, the elegant tapering of its spire. He wrote later, 'Does not the cathedral look very beautiful amongst the golden foliage; its silvery grey must sparkle in it?' Again, of the view from the tower of Fonthill, he would write: 'Salisbury, at fifteen miles off, darted up into the sky like a needle.'

During that first visit to Salisbury, Constable was depressed because his courtship of Maria Bicknell was being opposed by her family. As a result, and as he afterwards admitted, he had not done as much work as he might while he was there. Nonetheless, although he did not use oils, he made a number of drawings of the Cathedral and the surrounding country. Readers of *Martin Chuzzlewit* will recall that in Mr Pecksniff's work-room were drawings by the pupils of 'Salisbury Cathedral from the north. From the south. From the east. From the west. From the south-east. From the nor'-west.' Constable encompassed most of these aspects, and in one of his drawings anticipated by nine years his first rendering in oils of the view of the Cathedral seen from the Bishop's garden (fig. 31).

But the event which made the visit a true epoch in Constable's life was his meeting with the Bishop's nephew, another

Figure 32 *Salisbury Cathedral from the Close* (August, 1820).
This painting shows, on the left, a glimpse of the Bishop's Palace.
Canvas, Victoria & Albert Museum, London

John Fisher. Also a churchman, this John Fisher was twelve years younger than the artist. An immediate and deep sympathy sprang up between the two men, and the friendship which now developed had a far-reaching influence on the future of Constable's art. Because he felt able to write to the younger Fisher without any self-consciousness or false modesty, the correspondence between the two friends which has survived is the most precious source of information we have about the motives and roots of Constable's painting.

For the next few years contacts between the artist and both the Bishop and his nephew were maintained by London visits and in correspondence. John Fisher the younger was kept informed of the tortuous progress of his friend's courtship of Maria Bicknell and encouraged him to take the decisive step of marrying her.

When Constable finally made up his mind, Fisher wrote that he held himself 'ready and happy' to marry them. The wedding service took place at St Martin-in-the-Fields in October 1816, and Fisher invited the couple to spend part of their honeymoon in his country rectory at Osmington, on the Dorset coast. The Constables paid two brief visits to Bishop Fisher in Salisbury *en route*; a few drawings but no oil sketches are known to have been made then. In the following year the younger John Fisher became Archdeacon of Berkshire.

Surrounded by the warmth of family affection (his first son was born in 1817), Constable felt able to produce more ambitious work. He inaugurated this phase by sending to the Academy, in 1819, *The White Horse*, the first of a series of six-foot canvases in which he sought to embody both the poetry and the truth of the scenery of the Stour Valley in which

Figure 33 *Salisbury Cathedral from the Bishop's Grounds* (1823). The finished version, commissioned by Bishop Fisher, of the Ottawa sketch. The Bishop objected to the 'black cloud' in the summer sky. Canvas, Victoria & Albert Museum, London

he was born. This painting was large and original enough to attract favourable notice; its success led to his election as an Associate of the Royal Academy in the same year. Furthermore, the younger John Fisher bought the painting from the exhibition, an act of genuine appreciation at a time when Constable was still finding difficulty in selling his work.

This action was an auspicious prelude to the third of Constable's journeys to Salisbury in 1820, a journey which is central to the present theme. His host was the Archdeacon who, having recently become Canon residentiary, had moved into a house in Salisbury Close called Leydenhall. Constable and his wife now had the responsibility of two young children; all four were accommodated by Fisher for the greater part of July and August of that year. This was the only occasion when the complete family were together in Salisbury, and their presence contributed to make the visit both relaxed and productive.

When urging Constable to stay with him in the previous year, Fisher had written: 'As I have painting materials here of every sort, you have only to put yourself into the Mail any day

& come down hither.' These materials were available because Fisher, like his uncle the Bishop and his cousin Dorothea, was a keen amateur artist, and their scope gave his guest an unusual freedom.

Normally, Constable sketched in the open air on relatively small pieces of paper or mill board which he could fit into the lid of his paint-box. Fisher's stores enabled him to work from the motif on stretched canvases, some of which rivalled in size the paintings he would send for exhibition. Had it not been for Fisher's enthusiasm, Constable would not have set out to paint in the open air on canvases the size of *Salisbury Cathedral and Leydenhall from the River* (fig. 36) and *Salisbury Cathedral from the Bishop's Grounds*.

A number of dated drawings in two sketch-books give a good idea of how Constable spent these two summer months. He visited Stonehenge on 15 July and stayed for a few days between 28 July and 4 August in Gillingham, Dorset, a small country town of which Fisher had recently become Vicar. He was in the New Forest on the latter date. The remaining time

Figure 34 *Salisbury Cathedral from the Bishop's Grounds* (1826). The final version,
painted for the Bishop, with the offending black cloud removed.
Canvas, © the Frick Collection, New York

seems to have been spent largely in Salisbury, and we find Constable making careful pencil drawings of the Cathedral on 20 July and 22 August, and more distant views at the end of July and on 9 August. There is less direct evidence about the sketches he made in oil. A view of the Cathedral including, on the left, a side of the Bishop's Palace is dated August 1820.

That we can with some certainty associate at least four or five other oil sketches with the same visit, including the Ottawa sketch, is due in part to their stylistic consistency with this dated work. Another factor is the presence of green foliage; he did not pay another long summer visit to Salisbury till 1829.[2] The third tantalizingly ambiguous piece of evidence for Constable's activity in oils at the time is a single phrase in the first letter he wrote to John Fisher after his return, on 1 September. This reads: 'My Salisbury sketches are much liked – that in the palace grounds – the bridges – & your house from the meadows – the moat – &c.'

Out of this list 'your house from the meadows' can be firmly identified with the large sketch on canvas showing, on the right, Leydenhall and Archdeacon Fisher's garden, with the spire of the Cathedral beyond, seen across the River Avon (fig. 36). It demonstrates the assurance which Constable now brought to painting in the open air, even on a scale larger than usual. It might well be supposed that the sketch 'in the palace grounds' was a clear reference to the Ottawa picture. But this identification cannot be regarded as absolutely certain, since the small oil sketch made in August 1820, and now in the Victoria & Albert Museum (fig. 32), is equally taken from the Bishop's grounds. 'The moat' mentioned in the same list might refer to the upright sketch in the Fitzwilliam Museum, a summer view which shows, in the foreground, the stream which drains the Bishop's fishpond. Just possibly, however, it might refer to the Ottawa sketch, which shows the same channel at a different point. This stream was generally known to the Bishop's family as the 'canal', a term which Constable himself was fond of applying to his home-waters of the River Stour.

In any case there is a specific reference to the sketch *Salisbury Cathedral from the Bishop's Grounds* a month later. It is contained in a letter to Constable from the Bishop's elder daughter

Figure 35 *Salisbury Cathedral from the Bishop's Grounds* (1823).
The 'wedding present' picture, painted for the Bishop's younger daughter, Elizabeth.
Canvas, Henry E. Huntington Library and Art Gallery, San Marino, California

Dorothea, or 'Dolly', Fisher. She had been Constable's pupil since 1818, and kept him well occupied with her visits to his studio, her requests for the purchase of artists' materials, and her instructions for the framing and transport of her own paintings and copies of other masters. When she was writing on 8 October 1820 to thank Constable for sending a frame, she added: 'Papa desires me to say, he hopes you will finish for the Exhibition the view you took from our Garden of the Cathedral by the waterside....' Embodying as it does three elements in the composition which do not occur together in any other sketch – the Cathedral, the Bishop's garden, and the water-course in that garden – it must refer to the recently rediscovered sketch, now in Ottawa.

Dolly Fisher's letter shows that the Bishop approved the design of this sketch, and thought that if it were to be given further elaboration in the detail it would be of sufficient conse-quence for inclusion in the Royal Academy exhibition of 1821. He has not said definitely that he would buy it in a completed state, though there is a strong hint that this was his intention. In any event, Constable had for the moment other plans for his exhibition pictures. He intended to continue his series of large paintings of the Stour, and was attempting to complete an ambitious canvas of the opening of Waterloo Bridge by the Prince Regent, a task he did not achieve till 1832.

In November 1821, Constable went for a fourth visit to Salisbury, this time without any of his family. During a three-week stay he visited Winchester and did some drawings; but he does not seem to have paid any special attention to the views from the Bishop of Salisbury's garden. (It was of course too late in the year for the summer mornings which he preferred to

Figure 36 *Salisbury Cathedral and Leydenhall from the River* (1820). One of the larger studies
which Constable painted in the open air. Canvas, National Gallery, London

render in oils.) Next spring the Bishop reopened the question
by visiting the artist's studio. He was in East Bergholt, and Mrs
Constable wrote on 11 May 1822: 'He [the Bishop] rummaged
out the Salisbury & wanted to know what you had done.'

Six months later the Bishop wrote to Constable, expressing
his disappointment that he had not felt able to make a trip to
Salisbury that year because 'I was in hopes you would have
taken another *peep* or *two* at the view of our Cathedral from my
Garden near the Canal. But perhaps you retain enough of it in
your memory to finish the Picture which I hope will be ready to
grace my Drawing Room in London.' In reply, Constable
confirmed that he was undertaking a picture of the scene; a firm
commission had at last been given and accepted.

Archdeacon John Fisher had drawn Constable's attention to
the Bishop's love of patronage. But neither this firmly marked

trait nor his undoubted affection for his young protégé had led
to his giving a significant number of orders for his work. He
had commissioned a portrait of himself on the first Salisbury
visit of 1811, and ordered a replica for the Bishop's Palace at
Exeter. But he showed no desire to possess one of those Suffolk
landscapes which expressed the painter's deepest emotions, and
which would have reminded him of his former living at Langham. When at length he did bespeak a landscape, his order was
very much in the tradition of eighteenth-century patronage. He
wanted an exact topographical rendering of an edifice as per-
sonally associated with him as a country house was with its
owner: his Cathedral.

It is fair to say that the relatively few commissioned landscapes Constable had so far painted were almost all country-
house portraits. The earliest was *Old Hall, East Bergholt*, painted

for the Squire of East Bergholt in 1801. This was followed eight years later by his early masterpiece, *Malvern Hall,* painted for Henry Greswolde Lewis. In 1816, when he needed extra money to meet the expenses of his approaching marriage, he undertook a view of Wivenhoe Park, the seat of his friend, General Francis Slater-Rebow. The main exception to this series of architectural 'portraits' was occasioned by Thomas Fitzhugh, who wanted his bride, Philadelphia Godfrey, to take with her a painting of the Suffolk scenery, with which she had been familiar since her childhood. This imaginative request resulted in the panoramic *The Stour Valley and Dedham Village* (1816),[3] in the Museum of Fine Arts, Boston.

Possibly the Bishop was encouraged to employ Constable on a landscape by his nephew's purchase of *The White Horse.* In any case, once he had made up his mind, he was impatient to have the picture completed and exhibited. His original plan was that Constable should work up the Ottawa sketch to a higher degree of finish, but the painter did not accept this idea. Constable never wished to dispose of his sketches, which he regarded as the most valuable contents of his studio. As Redgrave recalled, 'He [Constable] used to say . . . that he had no objection to part with the corn, but not with the field that grew it.'[4]

In transferring the composition to a new canvas, Constable enlarged its dimensions by roughly one-quarter. Scale was always important to him, and he had a particular reason for wanting the impact of his picture to be as strong as possible. As he had been prevented by illness from completing a Stour scene or his *Whitehall Stairs: The Opening of Waterloo Bridge* (1832), the *Salisbury Cathedral from the Bishop's Grounds* was to be his main exhibit in the 1823 Academy. This is the version now in the Victoria & Albert Museum (fig. 33). It will be seen that, while he has followed the sketch closely, he has added the figures of the Bishop and his wife in the left foreground, and has taken considerable care over the architectural detail. That was the feature of the painting which gave him most concern, and made the completion of the painting in time for exhibition a matter of acute anxiety to him.

He wrote to the younger Fisher after the exhibition opened: 'My Cathedral looks very well. Indeed I got through that job uncommonly well considering how much I dreaded it. It is much approved by the Academy and moreover in Seymour St. [the Bishop's London house] though I was at one time fearfull it would not be a favourite there owing to a *dark cloud* – but we got over the difficulty, and I think you will say when you see it that I have fought a better battle with the Church than old Hume, Bro[u]gham and their coadjutors have done. It was the most difficult subject in landscape I ever had upon my easil [sic]. I have not flinched at the work, of the windows, buttresses, &c,

&c, but I have as usual made my escape in the evanescence of the chiaroscuro.'

Constable was highly conservative in his political views, and his reference to the radical thinkers Joseph Hume and Lord Brougham would be appreciated by Fisher, who was firmly opposed to any reform of the established Church of England.

As he implies, the detailed painting of a building always gave Constable the problem of how to combine literal accuracy with his personal approach to landscape. In this case he relied on the 'evanescence of the chiaroscuro'. The bold treatment of the buttresses and windows and the forceful contrasts of light and shade in the sketch are softened, the impact of the trees is made lighter by the definition of their leaves, and the Cathedral is more detached from the foreground by the light falling on it, and by these variations in emphasis.

The relation of an edifice to a landscape did not cease to plague him after the success of this painting. In 1833 he exhibited *Englefield House* in the Academy. When told by the President of the Royal Academy that it ought to be with the Architectural drawings as it was 'only the picture of a house', he retorted that it was 'a picture of a summer morning including a house'. Even so, he had complained, 'My house tires me very much. The windows and window frames and chimneys and chimney pots are endless.' If he felt this weariness about a Tudor mansion of moderate size, we can imagine the resolution he must have brought to bear on painting Salisbury Cathedral, which legend credits with 365 windows and as many pillars as there are hours in the year. He never forgot the labour it had cost him and wrote to a prospective purchaser when it was back on his hands, 'The time expended on it was enormous for its size'.

When the 1820 sketch was received in the National Gallery of Canada, it was X-rayed, with the fascinating result that Constable was seen to have commenced his painting with the canvas at right angles to its present direction (fig. 37). In the underlying layer of pigment the tower and spire can be seen crossing their final position at right angles, near the top of the spire in the later paint surface. There can be no question that the artist originally painted a vertical sketch of the same dimensions as we see today. However, in turning the canvas to begin the actual horizontal composition, now in Ottawa, he enlarged the painting by about an inch at the top.

He was at this period of his career prepared to interchange vertical and horizontal concepts of a scene; in 1824 his chief exhibit, *A Boat Passing a Lock*, was in a vertical format, and two years later he converted this into the horizontal format of his Diploma picture. The sketch in the Fitzwilliam of the spire seen above the close wall is a vertical design of the same group as the Ottawa sketch.

As he finally conceived it, the view shows the whole expanse of the southern face of the Cathedral and its roof. The octagonal building in front of and slightly to the right of the spire is the Chapter House, which is joined to the main fabric by the low wall running west to the Cloisters, themselves almost obscured by the trees in the left foreground. Its exhibition in the Academy of 1823 was far from marking the end of Constable's labours on the commission. The Bishop's younger daughter, Elizabeth, was to be married in the autumn of 1823, and he ordered a smaller version as a wedding present to greet her on her return from her honeymoon. This is the version now in the Huntington Library and Art Gallery, San Marino (fig. 35).

Figure 37 An X-ray of the Ottawa sketch which clearly reveals that Constable began his work at right angles to its present direction. In other words, it was originally intended to be a vertical painting.

Furthermore, Constable's remark, already quoted, that his painting might not have been a favourite 'owing to a dark cloud', is the first hint of a problem which occupied him till the Bishop's death in 1825, and even beyond. What is most interesting in relation to the Ottawa sketch is that the sky to which the Bishop objected, though somewhat less dramatic in impact, closely follows the shape of the clouds and the balance between light and shade in Constable's original draft. This was clearly the sky that he had actually observed, comparable in its implications of a forthcoming summer storm with the sky in *Salisbury Cathedral and Leydenhall from the River* (1820). As Fisher said of the exhibited picture, 'The spire sails away with the thunder-

clouds.' It has the same actuality as the skies which Constable had deliberately set out to study in Hampstead between 1820 and 1822. But the Bishop, whose taste had been formed by the 1770s, could not accustom himself to this lack of serenity. Archdeacon Fisher reported his lament: '[If] Constable would but leave out his black clouds! Clouds are only black when it is going to rain. In fine weather the sky is blue.'

It was one of the curious paradoxes in Constable's nature that although he could not bear being under an obligation to anyone, and fretted at firm dates for commissions, he would attend to suggestions from almost any visitor to his studio for alterations to the work he had in hand. This docility was evident in his later dealings with the Bishop over his *Salisbury Cathedral from the Bishop's Grounds* (fig. 33). In 1824 Dr Fisher asked Constable to call on him and, as the artist recorded, told him that 'he thought of my improving the picture of the Cathedral and mentioned many things. He hoped I would not take his observations amiss. I said, "Quite the contrary as his Lordship had been my kind monitor for twenty-five years."'

The version he ultimately delivered in response to the Bishop's proposals for improvement is that now in the Frick Collection, New York (fig. 34). The unfinished version in the Metropolitan Museum of Art, New York, may be his trial run for the picture in the Frick, or intended for yet another commission which did not mature. In the main, the alterations in the revised painting amount to a modification in the sky to make it less stormy in effect, the separation of the two taller foreground trees so that they no longer meet in an arch over the spire, and an increased sharpness of focus in the detailing of the architecture, accounted for by the sunnier light. The top right-hand corner now reveals a strip of blue sky and white cloud.

In this period of revision Constable also had the 'wedding present' picture back to introduce similar modifications in the effect of light. This introduction of what, in another context, he called 'eye-salve' was not completed until after the Bishop's death in 1825, but appears to have stilled the objections so far as his family was concerned. So full was Constable's studio of variants of the design that he recorded a remark of his daughter Minna that he was at work on 'three Cathedrums'.

When the work now in Ottawa was lent by Louis Huth to a Winter Exhibition organized by the Royal Academy in 1884, it was recognized as the sketch for the exhibited version of 1823. But, until its recent rediscovery, the only oil which could have been regarded as a potential sketch for the painting was that in a private collection.[5] Lightly rubbed in with dull colour and squared for transfer, this is clearly the preliminary for some more completed version.

It differs from all the finished versions by the inclusion of the tree masking the Chapter House and the south-east transept. In this respect, it follows the drawing which Constable had made of the scene during his first visit in 1811 (fig. 31). That drawing has itself been regarded as a preliminary stage in the 1823 painting. But closer examination shows that it is drawn from a point nearer to the water's edge. For the foreground trees, the angle of vision, and the staffage of cows, the exhibited picture need depend solely on the 1820 oil sketch. There is no certain evidence that in making that oil sketch Constable did not suppress a still existing tree. Certainly, even if it were not still there, he would have felt tempted to introduce it, to reduce the extent of his battle with the buttresses, windows and mouldings of the Gothic architecture. But truth, or the will of his patron, prevailed.

In the light of the reappearance of the Huth study, the sketch in a private collection is now seen to be in more likelihood an intermediate stage between the exhibited version of 1823 and the 'wedding present', which is of the same size as the sketch. It would be another example of Constable's practice of painting a study the same size as the definitive version, satisfying himself about the problems posed by a reduction in scale and, in this case, the change in mood imposed by the sunnier light.

The cult of ruins was felt strongly in Britain in the seventeenth century, and by the end of the eighteenth century the veneration of antiquities provided a main source of subject-matter for landscape painters. But Constable did not approach the painting of Salisbury Cathedral in the spirit of an antiquarian concerned with the rich tapestry of medieval thought. As the oil sketch shows, his first conception of the scene from the Bishop's garden was that the church formed a splendid background closing a pastoral and sylvan vista. It is almost as though he had come upon it by chance during a walk through country lanes and woods. When he painted his exhibition picture from the sketch, he undertook to emphasize the impact of the Cathedral in that setting, and to sharpen the detail, because of his affection for his patron and for the place.

His feelings about Gothic architecture were ambivalent. He said in his last lecture at Hampstead in 1836 that the intentions which led to the creation of medieval art were unknown to the modern age, and that a Neo-Gothic building is 'little less absurd than a new ruin'. Yet he was enchanted by Fonthill, that secular abbey in which Wyatt, after despoiling the interior of Salisbury Cathedral by his restorations, had as it were rebuilt it after his heart's desire for William Beckford. 'Imagine,' wrote Constable after seeing Fonthill, 'Salisbury Cathedral … magnificently fitted up with crimson and gold, and ancient pictures, and statues in every niche…. It is a strange, ideal, romantic place; quite fairyland.' But when he painted the exterior of the Cathe-dral, he did not try to anticipate the Pre-Raphaelite romanticizing of the past; he made of it a picture of a summer morning, including a cathedral. It was poetical with a poetry of his own devising, not heavily dependent on historical associations.

The question of the relationship between his sketches and his exhibited works is often discussed. In assessing them it must not be forgotten that he made two kinds of sketches. One was the open-air study, in which he sought to fix the transient aspects of what was immediately in front of him, the atmosphere, the accents of light on the foliage, the figures and animals who happened to be on the scene. The other type is the studio sketch, in which he worked out, generally on the same scale as the picture he finally planned, the precise structure and content of a composition, working from his open-air sketches of skies and weeds, enlarging landscape studies, and introducing a greater precision of design. His famous full-scale sketches for *The Hay Wain* (1821) and *The Leaping Horse* (1824) are examples of this latter kind. It is a type which contains more intellectual resource; but the open-air sketches have more immediacy, and generally more brilliance of effect.

The Ottawa sketch is exceptional in marrying the characteristics of both sorts of study. It embodies an almost immediate apprehension of the appearances before the artist's eyes. At the same time, the abnormally large scale on which he has painted his sketch from the motif gives it the status of a studio preliminary for the exhibited picture. As we have seen, it was in that light that the Bishop always regarded it.

When he hung his 'wedding present' picture in Seymour Street, Constable wrote, 'It will be better liked than the large one, because it is not "too good".' Even in the version he exhibited, the immediacy of his original concept has been partially diluted through the attention he had had to pay to architectural detail. The vivid freshness of his first impression is most effectively combined with the monumentality of his design in the sketch he made in 1820, now in Ottawa.

[1] Pluralism, or the holding of one or more benefices (church livings) at a time, was common in those days.
[2] He spent four days there in 1823, from 19 to 22 August, on his way to stay with Fisher at Gillingham, but is only known to have made one pencil sketch at Salisbury during this brief visit.
[3] Philadelphia was the daughter of Peter Godfrey, Lord of the Manor of Old Hall, East Bergholt, who had previously shown a warm interest in Constable's career.
[4] Richard and Samuel Redgrave, *A Century of Painters of the English School*, 1866, p. 396.
[5] Reproduced, when on loan to the City Art Gallery, Birmingham, in *Constable*, by Basil Taylor (Phaidon, second edition 1975), plate 87.

Richard Parkes Bonington, *View of the Grand Canal, Venice*, 9×13½ inches,
Yale Center for British Art, Paul Mellon Collection, 1971

Richard Parkes Bonington, *Off the French Coast*, 14×20 inches,
Private Collection, USA, 1980

Joseph Mallord William Turner, R.A., *Châteaux de St Michael, Bonneville, Savoy*,
35¾×48 inches, Yale Center for British Art, Paul Mellon Collection, 1978

Figure 38 Joseph Mallord William Turner, R.A., *Ostend*, 36×48 inches,
Neue Pinakothek, Munich, 1975

Turner's *Ostend*

EVELYN JOLL

It has for so long now been generally accepted that Turner's contribution to landscape painting was, in many ways, innovatory, that it is sometimes overlooked that whatever changes he introduced only came about after a thorough grounding in the art of his precursors in European painting. The artists to whom he paid most attention were Titian, Rembrandt, Willem van de Velde, Cuyp, Jacob Ruisdael, Nicolas Poussin and, above all, Claude. He studied their styles and methods so thoroughly that echoes of their work can be detected in Turner's paintings until almost the end of his life. Recollections of Claude's seaports, for example, persist in Turner's work into the late 1830s, while, in the early 1840s, Turner seems to have been attracted afresh by Titian and the Venetians and in 1844, the year in which *Ostend* (fig. 38) was exhibited, Turner paid his final homage to the Dutch marine tradition.

In view of this continuing thread of the work of Turner's predecessors in Europe running through his own, it is all the more extraordinary that Turner's pictures have been, at least until very recently, almost wholly neglected on the Continent. There is only one painting by him in a private collection in the whole of Europe (Belgium) and no Turner oil in any public collection in Austria, Belgium, Greece, Holland, Italy, the USSR, Spain or Switzerland. The Louvre acquired its only Turner painting as late as 1967 when it stopped the export to Mr Paul Mellon of *Landscape with a River and a Bay in the Distance* which had been in the Groult collection in Paris since at least 1890. It is against this background that the acquisition of *Ostend* by the Neue Pinakothek, Munich assumes particular importance. It is, so far, the only Turner painting in Germany whereas, by contrast, German museums own thirteen paintings by Claude.

The facile explanation usually put forward for this neglect of Turner on the Continent is that he was regarded there primarily as a watercolourist, a branch of art considered in some European circles in the nineteenth century as more suited to the amateur than to the professional painter. But more concrete reasons than this are surely required to explain why Turner's paintings failed to appeal to European collectors, and, in the case of Germany at least, some evidence on this very question is available, for it so happens that Turner's *Opening of the Walhalla 1842* was shown at the Congress of European Art in Munich in 1845. In fact, this was the only painting Turner sent to an exhibition outside Britain during his lifetime, for the three pictures he exhibited in Rome in 1828 had been painted while Turner was living there. Dr Christoph Heilmann who published an article on *Ostend* in *Pantheon* (xxxiv, 1976, pp. 221–30) has collected reports of almost universal condemnation of *Walhalla* in 1845: apart from its topographical liberties, hardly likely to commend it to a German audience, the critics considered its chief faults lay in its lack of drawing and, above all, in its mishmash of colours. Indeed, it is not difficult to understand why *Walhalla* found no admirers among those brought up to revere the currently popular Cornelian style.

There is also additional evidence to prove that Turner's work in oil did not appeal to German taste. The German painter Joseph Anton Koch (1786–1839), who had been in Rome in 1828–9 when Turner exhibited *Orvieto, Medea* and *Regulus* there, was among Turner's fiercest critics, publishing a scathing attack on Turner in *Moderne Kunstchronik* in 1834 and it was very likely he, according to Dr Heilmann, who first mentioned Turner to King Ludwig and doubtless did so in the most unflattering terms. Furthermore the great Dr Waagen was equally hostile, although he had gone to England prepared to admire Turner as he already knew his work through the medium 'of beautiful steel engravings'. When, however, he came face to face with *Ehrenbreitstein* at the R.A. Exhibition in 1835, he was appalled at 'such looseness, such a total want of truth, as I had never before met with. He has here succeeded in combining a crude, painted medley with a general foggy appearance.'

These opinions combine to suggest in part why 130 years separated the exhibition in Munich of *Walhalla* and the city's acquisition of *Ostend*.

In 1844 Turner sent seven pictures, including *Ostend*, for exhibition at the Royal Academy, one more than he had ever sent previously and a number equalled only in 1846. It is tempting to see in this burst of activity in the mid-1840s a last creative outpouring on Turner's part. How does it accord with Ruskin's report that Turner's health began to show signs of decline in 1845? There is, at any rate, not the slightest hint of this in his 1844 exhibits which show him, in his seventieth year, still at the very height of his powers. As the critic of the *Library of the Fine Arts* had written as long ago as 1831, 'When will Mr Turner show symptoms of decay?... his genius is still green as when we first saw it in the boyhood of our life'.

Ostend was bought by H. A. J. Munro of Novar, Turner's most prolific patron at this time, who bought a high proportion of the Academy exhibits that Turner sold between 1836 and 1844. *Ostend* is recorded as hanging in Munro's London house in Grosvenor Square in 1847 and was included in his sale at Christie's on 24 March 1860 (151) where it was bought by the dealer Ernest Gambart (1814–1902). There is then a gap of about thirty years in the picture's history until it was bought by Cornelius Vanderbilt II (1843–99). According to C. F. Bell it was 'bought by Mr Vanderbilt, without a pedigree, as a picture of Boulogne Harbour. Mr Thomas Moran, N.A. (1837–1926), first suggested that it was most probably the picture of Ostend exhibited in 1844'. As Gambart was acquainted with the Vanderbilt family and as Cornelius Vanderbilt II was only seventeen at the time of Munro's sale, it seems certain that Gambart sold the picture elsewhere in the 1860s. The picture then appears to have 'lost' its exhibited title and is not heard of again until 1889 when a Turner oil entitled *Fishing Boats in Boulogne Harbour, Storm Coming on* was lent to an exhibition at Whitechapel (no. 97) by T. C. Farrer. No dimensions are given in the catalogue, but the description is as follows: 'The entrance to the harbour is narrow and the lighthouse shows the bar of sand which makes the waves break. Turner has waited for a moment of a sudden squall, and has caught and fixed it on his canvas. The wind rushes, the sand hurries across the sky, the waves rage and tremble, and we feel the power that lives and works in nature.'

Although this description does not fit *Ostend* in every particular, it has a sufficient number of telling points in common with it to make it very likely that the picture exhibited at Whitechapel was in fact *Ostend*, especially when other pieces of evidence are taken into account. Although this is only conjecture, it appears probable that it was acquired by Cornelius Vanderbilt soon after being shown at Whitechapel as it was *c.*1890 that he bought another Turner oil, *Venice, from the Porch of Madonna della Salute* (now in the Metropolitan Museum, New York), from Lord Dudley, as well as the large watercolour of *Bamburgh*. So it is clear that Vanderbilt was interested in acquiring Turners at just about the time of the Whitechapel exhibition. *Ostend* then descended from Cornelius Vanderbilt to his daughter, Countess Szechenyi; it was acquired from her heirs by Agnew's in 1972 and bought by the Munich gallery in 1975.

By way of a postscript to the provenance, there is one further point connecting *Ostend* with the picture exhibited as *Boulogne Harbour*: when Geoffrey Agnew first saw the picture in Countess Szechenyi's apartment in New York in the 1950s, she referred to it as *Boulogne*, which suggests that the picture's '1889 title' had not been entirely forgotten.

When Turner exhibited *Ostend* in 1844, it was hardly noticed by the critics, whose attention was focussed mainly on *Rain, Steam and Speed*. The *Spectator*, however, mentioned *Ostend* favourably, together with *Fishing Boats bringing a Disabled Ship into Port Ruysdael* (fig. 39, Tate Gallery no. 536), and considered that both pictures were 'magnificent seapieces, without exaggeration and in these scenes the general effect is all sufficient...' But Ruskin did not agree that the two pictures were of equal merit: whereas he ranked *Port Ruysdael* as among Turner's 'most perfect sea pictures', he found *Ostend* 'somewhat forced and affected', a verdict which today seems unusually off-course.

Turner often travelled via Ostend on his journeys to the Continent, so he knew the town well. As far as is known, no watercolour sketches for the composition exist, and Turner appears to have relied mainly on his memory, assisted by a number of pencil sketches of a very summary kind in sketchbooks in use at widely varying dates. Most of these pencil studies are reproduced in Dr Heilmann's article and provide striking evidence of how little in the way of detailed record Turner needed at this time to build up a finished composition.

Two questions of interest about *Ostend* remain unanswered. First, was the choice of subject Turner's own or was it suggested to him either by his dealer, Thomas Griffith, or by a patron? And second, is the picture to be regarded as a straightforward seascape with a port in the background, or did Turner intend to invest the subject with some further meaning?

On the first question, the only evidence is contained in a letter

Figure 39 Joseph Mallord William Turner, R.A., *Fishing Boats Bringing a Disabled Ship into Port Ruysdael*,
Tate Gallery, London

from Turner to Thomas Griffith, written on 1 February 1844, which ends as follows: 'and Pray tell me if the new Port Ruysdael shall be with fish only and if the new *marine* Pictures are to have Dutch Boats only?' The reference to 'the new marine pictures' is presumably to *Ostend* and to *Van Tromp, going about to please his masters* (fig. 40, Royal Holloway College Collection), which Turner must at that time have been preparing for the R.A. exhibition. Why should Turner be consulting Griffith about the contents of these three pictures? It is difficult to answer this with so little knowledge about the precise relationship between the two men but, despite the opinion of Ruskin's mother, given in 1838, that Griffith was 'dishonest in the common acceptation of the word', he seems in general to have been highly regarded and Turner certainly trusted him. This trust was probably strengthened by Griffith's part in the negotiations over finding buyers for the sets of Swiss watercolours in 1842

Figure 40 Joseph Mallord William Turner, R.A., *Van Tromp Going about to Please His Masters*,
Royal Holloway College, University of London

and 1843. Then, with the publication, also in 1843, of the first volume of *Modern Painters*, which led to a sudden and increased demand for Turner's work, Turner seems to have begun to rely more on Griffith as his agent. Part of the above-quoted letter concerns the problem of the condition of the paintings in Turner's studio, for Griffith had clearly been urging Turner to have a number of pictures put in order so that prospective buyers might be offered as wide a choice as possible. All this suggests that at this time Turner and Griffith were in close touch, and that Turner placed considerable reliance on Griffith's advice. Bearing this in mind, how should Turner's sentence about 'the new marine pictures' be interpreted? Does it imply that Turner was painting these pictures on commission for clients that Griffith had found? The recent publication of the *Collected Correspondence of J. M. W. Turner* has shown that more pictures were painted on commission in the 1830s and '40s than was previously known, so that the possibility of a commission here cannot be ruled out, yet the 1844 *Port Ruysdael* was apparently never sold, and it seems more likely that *Ostend* and *Van Tromp* were bought by Munro and Gillott respectively either at the R.A. or shortly afterwards, rather than being painted expressly for them. A more plausible explanation, therefore, is that Griffith had found Turner's sea pictures to be readily saleable and had advised him to paint more of them, perhaps going so far as to suggest these subjects to Turner, and even some of the details they should contain. After all, both *Port Ruysdael* and *Van Tromp* returned to themes treated before (was Bicknell possibly considering the purchase of the 1827 *Port Ruysdael* at the time of Turner's letter? – he certainly bought it the following month), and it may not be entirely fanciful to suggest that *Ostend* may be seen as being in the line of succession to a picture such as *Van Goyen looking out for a Subject* (Frick Collection), in which Antwerp features in much the same way as Ostend does here.

When *Ostend* was lent to the exhibition *William Turner und die Landschaft seiner Zeit* at Hamburg in 1976 (no. 132) the Director of the Kunsthalle, Dr Werner Hofmann, suggested that the real subject of the picture is 'Seascape, with Christ stilling the tempest', and Andrew Wilton in *The Life and Work of J. M. W. Turner* (1979) agrees that 'it is difficult to avoid reading a figure in one of the small boats as Christ'. While I have not looked at

the picture again with this theory in mind, I find it hard to accept. First, there is no sign anywhere of a halo or of a figure singled out by special lighting, whereas in *Christ driving the Traders from the Temple* (Tate Gallery, no. 5474) the figure of Christ is surrounded by an aura of light which makes Him instantly identifiable. Furthermore, is Turner likely to have treated this subject with quite so much licence? To transfer Juliet from Verona to Venice is one thing, but to move Christ from the Sea of Galilee to Ostend is surely quite another. And again, if Turner had intended this theme to be illustrated in *Ostend*, would he not have made some reference to it in the picture's title – which is in fact the shortest of all the titles of his exhibited works? Andrew Wilton argues that there is no reference to the 'Christ' motif in the catalogue because 'It was not necessary for Turner in the 1840s to press such an allusion'. But I believe that Turner, despite an occasional and light-hearted predilection for mysteriousness, wanted his pictures to be fully understood and accordingly chose titles for them that were as explicitly informative as possible. For these reasons I find Dr Hofmann's reading of the picture unacceptable.

On 20 September 1826 a powder-magazine exploded just outside Ostend, causing several deaths; Turner's father, knowing him to be in the area, seems to have been responsible for a rumour that Turner might have been among those injured. Could there be any echo of this affair in *Ostend*? The figures at the end of the groyne on the left appear to be showing almost exaggerated anxiety over the fate of the boat which has just entered the calmer waters at the harbour's mouth; could this be intended as an allusion to Turner's proximity to danger and the concern felt for his safety among his friends in England? This interpretation seems pretty far-fetched and one wonders if there is any justification for seeking such esoteric allusions in the picture. After all, painting the sea had been a lifelong preoccupation of Turner's and the number of seascapes in the Turner Bequest, painted between 1835 and 1845, prove that the fascination of the subject remained as strong for Turner at this date as it ever had been. Therefore there seems to be no real evidence for reading anything into *Ostend* beyond Turner, encouraged perhaps by Griffith, exploring once more a favourite theme and moreover one which had not only inspired some of his greatest pictures but had also proved highly successful in terms of sales.

Joseph Mallord William Turner, R.A., *A Mountain Scene, Val d'Aosta*,
36×48 inches, National Gallery of Victoria, Melbourne, purchased 1973

Sir John Everett Millais, Bart., P.R.A., *A Huguenot on St Bartholomew's Day*,
36½×24½ inches, the Makins Collection, 1972

Sir Edward Coley Burne-Jones, Bart., *The Garden of the Hesperides*,
47×38½ inches, Hamburger Kunsthalle, Hamburg, 1973

Sir Edward Coley Burne-Jones, Bart., *Laus Veneris*, 48×72 inches,
Laing Art Gallery, Newcastle, Tyne & Wear County Council Museums
Service, 1972

Walter Richard Sickert, A.R.A., *The Eldorado Music Hall, Paris*, 19×23¼
inches, The Barber Institute of Fine Arts, Birmingham University, 1968

Walter Richard Sickert, A.R.A., *The Beribboned Washstand*,
22×18¼× inches, Private Collection, Australia, 1974

Charles Conder, *The Balcony*, 18×24 inches,
Private Collection, England, 1978

Charles Conder, *An Orchard in Blossom*, 25×30 inches,
Mr William Bowmore, Newcastle, Australia, 1971

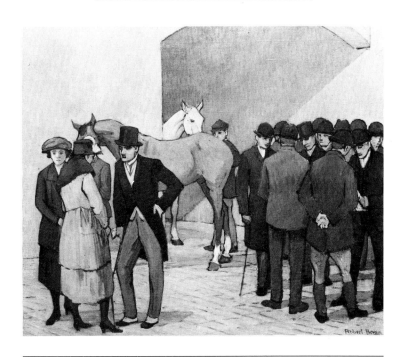

Robert Polhill Bevan, *A Morning at Tattersalls*, 28⅛×30⅛ inches,
from the collection of Mr Paul Mellon, Upperville, Virginia, 1969

Spencer Gore, *The Cinder Path*, 27×31 inches,
The Tate Gallery, 1975

160

Harold Gilman, *A Girl with a Teacup*, 24½×20¼ inches,
Private Collection, England, 1978

Baccio della Porta, called Fra Bartolommeo, *Study of the Kneeling Magdalen*, 8×5 inches, black chalk heightened with white, Private Collection, UK, 1980

Giulio Pippi called Giulio Romano, *Jupiter's Eagle Brings Psyche Water from the Styx*, 8¹⁄₈×15¹⁄₄ inches, pen and ink, Private Collection, England, 1975

Giuseppe Porta, called Il Salviati, *A Bearded Man*, 8×10³/₈ inches, coloured chalk, Private Collection, England, 1976

Annibale Carracci, *Two Studies of a Boy and Two of a Girl*, 8⁷/₈×12¹/₂ inches, red chalk, The Metropolitan Museum of Art, New York, Harris Brisbane Dick Fund and Rogers Fund, 1972

Giovanni Francesco Barbieri called Il Guercino, *A Fisherman with His Net*, 15¾×10⅞ inches, black chalk, National Gallery of Art, Washington, Pepita Milmore Fund, 1974

Federico Barocci, *Head of a Man*, 15½×10¾ inches, oil and paper laid down on canvas, The Metropolitan Museum of Art, New York, Harry G. Sperling Fund, 1976

Sir Peter Paul Rubens, *A Man in Chinese Dress*, 17⅝×9¾ inches,
black chalk heightened with red, Mr Alan Rofe, 1971, Private Collection,
USA, 1975

Jean Honoré Fragonard, *Rodomonte and Mandricardo State Their Case before Agramante*, 15×9½ inches, chalk, pen, ink and grey wash, The Museum of Fine Arts, Houston, Gift of General and Mrs Maurice Hirsch, 1978

Claude Gellée, called Le Lorrain, *Coastline of Santa Marinella*, 8¼×12¾ inches, pen and ink, Private Collection, England, 1977

Giovanni Antonio Canal, called Canaletto, *The Doge at St Maria della Salute*,
15×21¾ inches, pen, ink and wash, Private Collection, USA, 1975

Thomas Gainsborough, R.A., *Rustic Lovers*, 14×9¾ inches,
pen, ink and wash, Cabinet des Dessins, Musée du Louvre, Paris, 1976

Thomas Gainsborough, R.A., *Coastal Scene with Shipping, Figures and Cows*,
10⅜×13¾ inches, grey wash, Private Collection, USA, 1979

John Robert Cozens, *Greenwich*, 19½×27⅞ inches, watercolour,
Whitworth Art Gallery, University of Manchester, 1972

Thomas Girtin, *Kelso*, 10¹/₂×17³/₈ inches, watercolour,
Private Collection, England, 1978

John Constable, R.A., *A River at Sunset*, 4¹/₂×8³/₄ inches,
watercolour, Private Collection, England, 1976

Richard Parkes Bonington, *Dunkerque from the Sea*, 7³/₄×10¹/₄ inches,
watercolour, Private Collection, USA, 1977

Joseph Mallord William Turner, R.A., *Seelisberg*, 8¼×11 inches,
watercolour, Private Collection, England, 1976

Joseph Mallord William Turner, R.A., *Longships Lighthouse*, 11×17 inches,
watercolour, Private Collection, USA, 1980

Joseph Mallord William Turner, R.A., *Brunnen, Lake Lucerne*,
11⁷⁄₈×18¹⁄₄ inches, watercolour, Private Collection, England, 1968

Joseph Mallord William Turner, R.A., *Goldau*, 11⅝×18 inches,
watercolour, Private Collection, USA, 1978

Joseph Mallord William Turner, R.A., *The Pass of Faido, St Gotthard*, 11⅝×18¼ inches, watercolour, Collection of Eugene Victor Thaw, New York, 1979

Joseph Mallord William Turner, R.A., *The Lake of Lucerne: Fluelen Looking towards the Lake*,
Yale Center for British Art, Paul Mellon Collection, 1974

William Blake, *St Mary Magdalene at the Sepulchre*, pen, ink and water
colour, Yale Center for British Art, Paul Mellon Collection, 1971

Samuel Palmer, *The Towered City*, 20¼×27½ inches,
watercolour and body colour, The Rijksmuseum, Amsterdam, 1977

Figure 41 *Zal is sighted by a caravan*. Attributed to Abd ul-Aziz. Folio 62 from the Houghton
Shahnameh. Tabriz, *c*. 1525. Private Collection
Zal is born to Sam with the inauspicious feature of white hair. He is abandoned on Mount
Alburz to meet his fate, but there he is found and fostered by a giant and magical
bird, the Simurgh. From time to time a passing caravan would pause and wonder at this
strange sight, until increasing rumours reached the ears of Sam who later reclaims the boy

Miniatures from the Houghton *Shahnameh*

TOBY FALK

The Houghton manuscript of Firdausi's *Shahnameh* is universally recognized as one of the most magnificent of all oriental illustrated manuscripts. It was made for Shah Tahmasp, who reigned at Tabriz from 1524 to 1576, and represents a high point of Persian miniature painting under the Safavids.

From the start the manuscript enjoyed an illustrious history. The young Shah from his youth showed a great enthusiasm for painting and was himself an accomplished artist. He lavished personal interest and huge expense on the making of the manuscript, and we can only assume that much of the astonishing freedom of interpretation found in the illustrations was a result of his unfettering encouragement to his artists. One of the peculiar qualities which sets him aside from other great art patrons is his ability to blend keenness with patience. So many of the world's more ambitious art projects have succumbed to being spoiled by short cuts taken through impatience. In sixteenth-century Iran the peak achievements of master artists were found in the medium of manuscript illustration, and in the royal atelier all the most celebrated painters were gathered to work on one volume. This was the way to produce the very finest book for a king, and the ambience of top artists respectfully vying with each other created the captivating if highly specialized splendour of these paintings.

The text of the *Shahnameh*, Firdausi's poetical account of the history of Iran, makes a great play of the more daring and fanciful exploits of past kings. So the miniatures are of an essentially narrative nature, but each artist has in his enthusiasm extended his work far beyond the mere telling of a story. Each miniature represents an idealized view of a world of perfection, embellished with a wealth of anecdotal and natural detail. It is this contrast between the central narrative and minute observation which creates the special and intriguing quality of these pictures, at which a royal reader might pause and gaze with fascination and pride.

However, after the atelier had been at work on the *Shahnameh* for over twenty years, the project began to outlive Shah Tahmasp's ardour. He was overtaken by persistent political responsibilities, and his interest in painting receded, until by 1568 he was able to make the surprising sacrifice of giving the volume to Sultan Selim II of Turkey, the very country which had been giving him such trouble on his western borders. It remained in the Ottoman Library until the early years of this century, by which time it had been acquired by Baron Edmond de Rothschild, from whose descendants it was purchased in 1959 by the distinguished American bibliophile Arthur A. Houghton Jr.

During Rothschild ownership the manuscript had been little seen or publicized, and an aura of mystery had grown up around it. In the hands of Arthur Houghton the book has been opened to scholars and public through exhibitions and publications. In departing from their traditional concentration on European art, Agnew's have been able to contribute to the publicizing of this exceptional manuscript by taking part in the dispersal of some of the miniatures.

182

Figure 42 *Faridun tests his three sons.* Attributed to Aqa Mirak. Folio 42 from the Houghton
Shahnameh. Tabriz, *c.* 1535. Private Collection

Faridun, before dividing his kingdom between his sons, tests their characters by appearing as a fire-breathing dragon. The first youth flees, the second draws his sword with threats, but the third, Iraj, keeps his head and reasons with the monster on the futility of picking a fight with the sons of the feared Faridun

Figure 43 *Gushtasp slays the dragon on Mount Saqila.* Attributed to Mirza Ali.
Folio 402 from the Houghton *Shahnameh*. Tabriz, *c*. 1535. Private Collection
Gushtasp, while at the court of Constantinople, is inveigled into carrying out acts of daring on behalf of
the suitors of his sisters-in-law. The greatest act is to rid Mount Saqila of its dragon, and this he achieves
with the aid of a specially prepared poisoned dagger

184

Mosan, *c.* 1180, one of the pair of enamelled gilt-copper armillae
from the coronation vestment of the Emperor Frederick Barbarossa,
4½×5×1¾ inches, Germanisches Nationalmuseum, Nuremberg, 1978

The Master G. VDR, *Mr Hamlet Winstanley*, ivory, height 5½ inches,
Victoria & Albert Museum, purchased with the aid of
the National Art–Collections Fund, 1980

Antoine-Louis Barye, *A Horse Attacked by a Tiger*,
bronze, 14½×10¼×6½ inches,
Australian National Gallery, Canberra, 1980

Workshop of Andrea Briosco, called Riccio, *An Oil Lamp*,
bronze, height 4 inches, Private Collection, New York, 1979

Figure 44 Diego Rodriguez de Silva y Velasquez, *Juan de Pareja*, 32×27½ inches, Metropolitan Museum of Art, New York, Isaac D. Fletcher Fund, Rogers Fund & Bequest of Adelaide Milton de Groot (1876–1967), Bequest of Joseph H. Durkee, by exchange, supplemented by gifts from Friends of the Museum, 1971

Velasquez's
Juan de Pareja

GEOFFREY AGNEW

The story of the sale in 1970 of Velasquez's portrait of Juan de Pareja (fig. 44) has been only partially, and not always accurately, reported. Since this was a highly dramatic event and since the price fetched set an entirely new set of values for Old Master pictures during the following decade, I have thought it worth recording the story in full as far as Agnew's was involved.

In a sense it all began in Los Angeles at the County Museum which I visited with my wife and son, Julian, in September 1970. Sitting in the Director's office, our eyes were suddenly riveted by a photograph lying on his desk. To our astonishment it was the Radnor Velasquez, the portrait of the painter's mulatto servant Juan de Pareja, painted in Rome between 1649 and 1650, one of the most famous pictures in the world. The Director, Mr Donahue, told us it had just arrived from Christie's, who were to sell the picture for the new Lord Radnor in November.

This compounded our amazement. Clearly the auctioneers had informed all the important museums of the forthcoming sale before giving the news to their principal clients, the dealers. This was confirmed later that day by a call we made to London, where the news had just broken. The impending sale through Christie's was something of a shock to us. Agnew's had in 1948 acted for the late Lord Radnor in selling some pictures, including Poussin's *Crossing of the Red Sea*, now in the National Gallery of Victoria, Melbourne. On one occasion Lord Radnor had most generously lent us the Velasquez for an exhibition in aid of charity. We had, at his request, on several occasions valued the picture for insurance, the last time only a few years before his death.

We were in fact due to visit Longford on 12 November and it had been in my mind, ever since his father's death, that Lord Radnor might have heavy duties to pay and might find it necessary to sell a picture. If that picture was to be the Velasquez, one option open to him would be to negotiate a sale in lieu of duty with the Treasury, for it was evident that the picture must rank very high in the National Gallery's list of desiderata. Presumably the net result for Lord Radnor, if he dealt directly or in lieu of duty with the National Gallery, would have been a much larger sum than he would eventually have received by selling through auction, where the special tax remissions on works of art sold to museums in the United Kingdom did not apply. (It was afterwards rumoured that some 70 per cent of the price went, in fact, to the Treasury.)

Tom Hoving's account, in *The Chase, the Capture: Collecting at the Metropolitan*, published in 1975, of how Lord Radnor had made the decision to sell the Velasquez because of an attempted robbery does not fit in with what Lord Radnor told us during our visit on 12 November. The only direct reference that he made to his decision to sell was that, in order to pay death duties, he had had to decide between selling land or a picture. He felt that land would be of more value to his family in the future.

None of this, of course, was known until much later and it has never been known for certain whether, in fact, either before the announcement of the sale or afterwards, direct negotiations with the National Gallery of London took place. In Los Angeles that September, however, there was nothing to be done and we left shortly afterwards.

The memory of that photograph continued to haunt me. I knew the picture well and that it was in marvellous condition. It was a picture with a romantic history. Velasquez had been in Italy in 1649 and 1650, sightseeing and searching for pictures for his patron, Philip IV. His studio assistant and travelling companion had been Juan de Pareja. It seems that since Velasquez was due to start on his great portrait of Pope Innocent X, but had not touched a brush for several months, he had painted his servant in order to 'loosen up his fingers'. According to Palomino, the portrait was executed 'with such similitude and liveliness that having sent it by the same Pareja to some friends to pass their judgement on it, they stood a while looking sometimes on the picture and sometimes on the original with Amazement, and even a sort of Terror, without knowing which they were to speak to or which was to answer them'.[1] It was indeed 'life and truth, not just art', as had been said some 350 years before.

The picture had been brought to England in the eighteenth century by Sir William Hamilton, and although Hamilton had lost a great part of his collection of antiquities by shipwreck, most of his pictures reached London, having been saved by Nelson in the Foudroyant. Subsequently the painting had been sold at Christie's in 1831 for 39 guineas and had been acquired by Lord Radnor's ancestor some years later for approximately £150.

The sale was to be on 27 November. Our immediate task was to estimate what the picture might fetch. The highest price given at auction up to that time was £821,482 for Rembrandt's *Aristotle Contemplating the Bust of Homer*, a picture whose history was as complete as that of the Velasquez, having been commissioned from Rembrandt by Don Antonio Ruffo, a Sicilian nobleman. The Rembrandt had been bought in New York in 1961 at the Erickson sale by the Metropolitan Museum against the Cleveland Museum. Since then the National Gallery of Washington had bought, from the Prince of Liechtenstein's Collection, Leonardo's portrait *Genevra dei Benci*. This was a picture which Agnew's had long tried to buy for the National Gallery of Canada, an opportunity they had not been able to grasp. My guess was that Washington had eventually paid something like $5½ million. The price of the Leonardo, as it turned out, was to be a decisive factor in who was to be the eventual buyer of the Velasquez.

By mid-October there was great excitement in the London art world about the forthcoming sale. Everyone who knew the Velasquez felt that it was a picture that the National Gallery must have. It was true that Velasquez was richly represented there, and in the Wellington Museum at Apsley House, but none of the National Gallery's three portraits could be compared artistically with the Radnor portrait. Certainly there were many friends of the National Gallery who would have liked to contribute to its acquisition. But, although there were rumours that the National Gallery was trying to negotiate, nothing definite had emerged.

We had decided shortly after our return that whatever price had been given for the Leonardo was bound to a great extent to set the price for the Velasquez. We felt that although the Velasquez might be considered less valuable than the Leonardo, the difference could only be marginal. Meanwhile, we waited to see whether we were approached by any of our clients. Among American museums, the Metropolitan and Cleveland seemed very likely to bid for *Juan de Pareja*. As both these museums had bought pictures by Velasquez through Agnew's since the war, it seemed possible that one, or possibly both, would get in touch with us, but neither did so. In early November, however, Paul Mellon, Chairman of the National Gallery of Washington and son of its founder, contacted us. On learning that we were as yet uncommitted over the Velasquez, he asked me to fly to New York to confer with the Trustees about the possibility of acting for them.

I flew to New York on 9 November. As it happened my partner, Evelyn Joll, was in America at the time. He knew nothing of what had taken place in the last few days and was surprised, when I telephoned, to find me in New York. I asked him to meet me outside the Knickerbocker Club. For some time we paced the pavements of Fifth Avenue, discussing what price I should recommend. My idea up to that time had been a maximum of 2 million guineas, something like twice the price, I learnt afterwards, which had been expected by Christie's and by most experts. Evelyn was slightly doubtful if 2 million guineas would be enough and, although it seemed at the time a huge price, I was greatly influenced by his opinion.

The next morning I met Paul Mellon at his house in New York. Carter Brown, Director of the National Gallery of Washington, was also present, together with two of his Trustees. In the discussion that followed the prime question was, of course, what price the picture might fetch. We had discussed this very fully in London, but in view of Evelyn Joll's comments the previous night I had decided to recommend going to a bid over 2 million guineas. Closely connected with the price was the question of an export licence: it seemed certain that the National Gallery in London would object to the picture's export, but it might well prove impossible for them to raise a sum of this magnitude within three months, the period normally recommended by the Reviewing Committee.

Some time was also spent in considering who else might bid for the picture. With a picture of such quality the sum likely to be involved was beyond the resources of all but a handful of buyers. Besides the Metropolitan and Cleveland, already mentioned, the American museums likely to be most interested were Toledo and the Kimbell Foundation at Fort Worth, while in Europe Berlin, Munich and the Louvre were all potential buyers. Among private collectors Norton Simon and Baron Thyssen appeared as the most dangerous rivals, whereas it is perhaps of interest to record, in the light of subsequent history, that it was considered improbable that Paul Getty would bid for the Velasquez, a prediction that was to prove correct.

While I was marshalling the arguments in favour of the figure we recommended, I was dismayed to learn that the Trustees had already held a meeting at which they had decided to bid the dollar equivalent of 1,800,000 guineas. It also transpired that they had been in direct touch with Lord Radnor and had obtained his agreement that no payment need be made until an export licence was granted. This seemed to me, at the time, to have been an unwise move, revealing Washington's interest. It had been done, however, and in retrospect does not appear to have had any influence on the result. The meeting ended after the Trustees had agreed to let me know if they were prepared to increase their bid. A few days later Paul Mellon telephoned me in London to say that the Trustees had authorized a bid of $5.3 million (about 2,100,000 guineas).

There followed a period of very complicated planning. At the fall of the hammer the responsibility for insurance would be on the buyer. We therefore had to tell our insurance company that we might have to call on them at a moment's notice, but without, in the interests of security, giving any precise idea of the sum involved. After protracted negotiations the insurance company named the maximum sum they were prepared to cover, over £1 million but considerably less than the sum we had been commissioned to pay. On the very day before the sale the insurance company rang up to say that they had not been able to 'lay off' in the insurance market the figure they had agreed and could not, therefore, cover the picture at all. With the greatest difficulty they were persuaded to adhere to the figure promised, but it was a bad moment.

There were other arrangements to be made too: a fireproof security van for transportation (since the picture would be only partially insured during transit), a bank vault in which to deposit the picture and a strategy for dealing with sabotage; for example, if the picture were to reach an unprecedented sum a fanatic might easily have protested by throwing acid at the picture as it stood on the easel. We arranged for our Head Foreman to be ready behind the rostrum with a blanket to cover the picture immediately it was knocked down and to spirit it into Christie's back premises. As a decoy we planned to have the Agnew van draw up ostentatiously at the front door of Christie's shortly before the picture came up, while the security van was to be at Christie's back door. A secretary was stationed in a telephone booth at Christie's ready to call the insurance company directly the hammer fell.

There remained one further problem. Since there was no precedent for a picture fetching £1 million at auction, it was difficult to know what advances in bids the auctioneer would make. Five per cent was the general rule, but the auctioneer had the right to make what advances he wished. With an auctioneer who had been known to refuse a bid he did not consider a sufficient advance, the problem was a real one. Its importance lay in the decision as to when to enter the bidding. It would have been disastrous to come in on the wrong foot and find someone else making our final bid. After lengthy discussion we decided, correctly as it turned out, that over 1 million guineas the advances would probably be in 50,000 guineas and would remain so until 2 million guineas, when they might go up by 100,000-guinea bids at a time. It was important, therefore, that we should come in on the odd rather than the even bid. In that way, if our guess was correct, we could make the opposition bid 2 million guineas and ourselves advance to 2,100,000 guineas. On the other hand there was the danger that the auctioneer might interpret our bid as 2,050,000 guineas, in which case we should be on the wrong foot.

The day of the sale, 27 November, arrived. My partners and I set off for Christie's that morning, tense but with high hopes. We had tried to anticipate every contingency. With us we had the largest bid we had ever been given, a bid unprecedented in sale-room history. However, I knew the vagaries of auctions for good and bad and was fully aware that something unforeseen could occur.

It was a long wait for lot 110, the last lot in a two-hour sale which contained very little else that interested us. At one point we conferred again outside the room and made the final decision that if we were forced into a 50,000-guinea bid after 2 million guineas we would take the risk of throwing in our commission and bidding 2,150,000 guineas, trusting that Washington would accept the fact that we had exceeded their bid and would take our commission as a contribution towards the extra 50,000 guineas. In the glare of innumerable arc lights and with photographers lining both walls, the Velasquez was placed on the rostrum. I was determined to bid very slowly since I knew that the auctioneer would try to make the bidding fast. By bidding slowly I hoped to deflate the excitement, and to give time to the opposition to realize what huge sums they were risking. I aimed at making my first bid fairly late, at either 1,350,000 or 1,450,000 guineas. At that point I thought it would be unlikely that there would be more than one other bidder left, but it was also important at that stage to get the bidding into my hands.

Bidding started at 300,000 guineas. William Mostyn-Owen of Christie's (bidding, we surmised, for the Louvre) went up to

900,000 guineas. Hugh Leggatt, the London dealer, entered at 950,000 guineas, but fell out at 1,250,000. And here I must correct Tom Hoving's perhaps understandably somewhat self-congratulatory account of the bidding at the sale in *The Chase, The Capture*. The Metropolitan had commissioned Wildenstein, the New York dealers, to bid for them. According to Hoving, Wildenstein's first bid was 1,600,000 guineas. My impression was that they had been bidding earlier. The only alternative bidder that I can think of, after Leggatt fell out, would have been the Cleveland Museum since, according to Hoving, they bid up to 3,500,000 dollars. In any case I made my first bid at 1,450,000 guineas and was very relieved to be in on the right foot. From then on there were only two of us. Wildenstein's at 1,500,000, Agnew's 1,550,000 and so on, by 50,000-guinea rises, until Wildenstein's bid 2,000,000. At exactly the same pace I had maintained throughout I made my last bid of 2,100,000 guineas. Wildenstein capped it at 2,200,000 and, sadly, I said to Julian, 'Well, that is that.'

After a moment's pause, the auctioneer announced Wildenstein. It had taken exactly 130 seconds.

As we left the sale-room, commiserating with ourselves and trying to conjecture who the buyer could be, we passed Sherman Lee of Cleveland. It was obvious from his expression that it had not been Cleveland. Sadly, I remarked to Julian, who had always been rather more confident than myself: 'Well, I shall never live to buy a million-pound picture, but I am sure you will.' Sadly, we started to dismantle all our elaborate arrangements, the most complicated plan we had ever made, and for an operation which never came about. Sadly, I telephoned Paul Mellon and Carter Brown, for whom it was very early in the morning, and told them the news. They received it stoically, but with undisguised astonishment.

After the sale Alec Wildenstein (his father, Daniel Wildenstein, had awaited the result on the nearest piece of French territory at Prunier's restaurant) announced to the Press that in buying the Velasquez for Wildenstein's he had fulfilled the dream of his great-grandfather, Nathan Wildenstein, who had seen the picture once on a visit to England, had considered it one of the greatest pictures in the world and had always wished his firm to buy it. It seemed at the time that this might be an imaginative exaggeration in the excitement of the moment. Technically, however, it may have been true. Hoving describes how, eleven days before the sale, the Metropolitan had authorized Wildenstein to bid up to 'a sum not to exceed 2 million guineas plus one bid'. Normally, that would be interpreted as 2,100,000 guineas (the same bid I had already received from Washington). Hoving goes on to say that two days before the sale he and the President of the Metropolitan authorized Wil-

denstein to go to the next bid back to them, i.e. 2,200,000 guineas. Perhaps the confusion arose because the Metropolitan may have had to raise the additional 100,000 guineas before completing the purchase from Wildenstein's. With two bidders so nearly on the same mark one of them is inevitably the unlucky one.

Naturally, the sale created enormous publicity and widespread comment. As a well-balanced editorial in *The Burlington Magazine* put it, much of the comment was 'as usual, misinformed, prejudiced, irrelevant or plain silly'. The art critic of one newspaper said he burst out laughing when he heard the price and his laughter turned to disgust. Another commented that the 'art world, light years away from the world of the artist, has over-reached itself this time' and called the price 'preposterous'. *The Burlington Magazine*, however, pointed out that given inflation and the rapidly dwindling supply of such masterpieces 'the Velasquez may well seem a bargain by 1980', and recalled that £800,000 for the Royal Academy's Leonardo cartoon, although it seemed a lot in 1962, now looked cheap.

Inevitably there were cries of 'Save the Velasquez' for 'our national heritage' and there was talk of launching an appeal fund. One writer to the press neatly deflated the 'national heritage' theory by saying that he had not been around in 1801 for the 'Save the Velasquez for Italy' fund, with a target of 39 guineas, nor had he contributed to the 'Save the Velasquez for Spain' fund. He added he hoped he would not one day be faced with a 'Save the Velasquez for America' appeal.

Seriously and quite rightly the National Gallery issued a press release on 3 December which 're-affirmed their long-maintained conviction ... that it ought to be acquired for the collection at Trafalgar Square'. Their plea was backed by the Reviewing Committee, which recommended holding up the export licence until 22 March and urged the Government to make available the large sum of tax involved to help finance its purchase. But the shock had been too great. If only, before the sale, the National Gallery could have been assured of government support, Agnew's could have told Washington the position. They might then not have bid, in which case the price would have been 1,400,000 guineas. As it was the Government refused any help. No appeal was launched and the export licence was eventually granted.

From that moment, however, nothing has ever been quite the same in the art market. The £1 million work of art had arrived and what was more it was an Old Master picture and not an Impressionist. As *The Burlington Magazine* had prophesied, in the light of subsequent events (for example, the sale in 1980 of Turner's *Juliet and Her Nurse* for $7,040,000), the price of the Velasquez took on a different aspect. The rapid fall in the value of money during the decade and the dwindling supply of masterpieces had radically altered the price scale.

The sale of the Velasquez had further important results. It was, I think, generally realized that the 'long stop' of the Reviewing Committee was not always going to be enough. In future the Trustees of the National Gallery might have to make their own effort if they wished to acquire such high-priced pictures. And so, when Titian's *Diana and Actaeon* appeared at Christie's in 1971 and was sold for 1,600,000 guineas, the National Gallery, although unable to act before the sale, immediately launched an appeal. This was a beautiful picture, but it did not, in many people's opinion, compare in quality, condition or rarity with the Velasquez. Nevertheless, after some twelve months, the sum was raised. It had become clear that the Trustees of the National Gallery must themselves enter the market on certain occasions, even when export control operated, either by negotiating direct before the sale or by going to the sale itself. This became possible when, by the late 1970s, the Government accepted that the National Gallery must have a far larger allocation to spend as they wished. To rely on special grants for special occasions was too capricious a system. In this way the loss of the Velasquez was not all loss.

Now the Velasquez hangs in the Metropolitan Museum, beautifully cleaned and with $1\frac{3}{8}$ inches of the canvas at the top and $2\frac{1}{4}$ inches at the right, which had been folded over, revealed again, with great advantage to the spatial composition. Washington had lost a picture they badly needed. Agnew's can only record it here as 'the one that got away'. The National Gallery was deprived of a superb addition to the greatest collection of Velasquez's pictures outside the Prado. Unfortunately, there was only one *Juan de Pareja*.

---

[1] Palomino: *El Museo pictórico*. He gives a full, though not wholly accurate account of Velasquez's second journey to Italy.

Index